THE PIG
A British History

Above: Low's Wild Boar. It bears little resemblance to Youatt's (see p. 34), and, particularly because of the partially 'dished' frontal profile, is much more like the Neapolitan and other Mediterranean types, to which it is probably related. It is an interesting dark russet colour in the original illustration. *Below*: Low's Berkshire suggests that the traditionally black colour of that breed, allegedly traceable to the 1820s, was by no means the only colour found. The origins of the reddish hue shown in the original illustration are the subject of much controversy. From Low (1842).

THE PIG
A British History

Julian Wiseman

Duckworth

Second edition 2000
First published in 1986 under the title
A History of the British Pig by
Gerald Duckworth & Co. Ltd
61 Frith Street, London W1V 5TA
Tel: 0207 434 4242
Fax: 0207 434 4420
Email: enquiries@duckworth-publishers.co.uk

A catalogue record for this book is available
from the British Library

ISBN 0 7156 2960 3

Printed in Great Britain by
Ebenezer Baylis & Son Limited, Worcester

Contents

Dissertation upon Roast Pig

Charles Lamb

This humorous flight of fancy by the great English essayist, Charles Lamb (1775-1834), was written at a time when pig breeding was all the rage.

Mankind, says a Chinese manuscript, which my friend M. was obliging enough to read and explain to me, for the first seventy thousand ages ate their meat raw, clawing or biting it from the living animal, just as they do in Abyssinia to this day. This period is not obscurely hinted at by their great Confucius in the second chapter of his Mundane Mutations, where he designates a kind of golden age by the term Cho-fang, literally the Cooks' holiday. The manuscript goes on to say, that the art of roasting, or rather broiling (which I take to be the elder brother), was accidentally discovered in the manner following. The swine-herd Ho-ti having gone out into the woods one morning, as his manner was, to collect mast for his hogs, left his cottage in the care of his eldest son Bo-bo, a great lubberly boy, who being fond of playing with fire, as younkers of his age commonly are, let some sparks escape into a bundle of straw, which kindling quickly, spread the conflagration over every part of their poor mansion, till it was reduced to ashes. Together with the cottage (a sorry ante-diluvian make-shift of a building, you may think it), what was of much more importance, a fine litter or new-farrowed pigs, no less than nine in number, perished. China pigs have been esteemed a luxury all over the East, from the remotest periods that we read of. Bo-bo was in the utmost consternation, as you may think, not so much for the sake of the tenement, which his father and he could easily build up again with a few dry branches, and the labour of an hour or two, at any time, as for the loss of the pigs. While he was thinking what he should say to his father, and wringing his hands over the smoking remnants of one of those untimely sufferers, an odour assailed his nostrils, unlike any scent which he had before experienced. What could it proceed from? Not from the burnt cottage – he had smelt that before – indeed this was by no means the first accident of the kind which had occurred through the negligence of this unlucky young firebrand. Much less did it resemble that of any known herb, weed or flower. A premonitory moistening at the same time overflowed his nether lip. He knew not what to think. He next stooped down to feel the pig, if there were any signs of life in it. He burnt his fingers, and to cool them he applied them in his booby fashion to his mouth. Some of the crumbs of the scorched skin had come away with his fingers, and for the first time in his life (in the world's life, indeed, for before him no man had known it) he tasted – *crackling!* Again he felt and fumbled at the pig. It did not burn him so much now, still he licked his fingers from a sort of habit. The truth at length broke into his slow understanding, that it was the pig that smelt so, and the pig that tasted so delicious; and, surrendering himself up to the newborn pleasure, he fell to tearing up whole handfuls of the scorched skin with flesh next it, and was cramming it down his throat in his beastly fashion, when his sire entered amid the smoking rafters, armed with retributory cudgel, and finding how affairs stood, began to rain blows upon the young rogue's shoulders, as thick as hail-stones, which Bo-bo heeded not any more than if they had been flies. The tickling pleasure, which he experienced in his lower regions, had rendered him quite callous to any inconveniences he might feel in those remote quarters. His father might lay on, but he could beat him from his pig, till he had fairly made an end of it, when, becoming a little more sensible of his situation, something like the following dialogue ensued:

"You graceless whelp, what have you got there devouring? Is it not enough that you have burnt me down three houses with your dog's tricks, and be hanged to you, but you must be eating fire, and I know not what – what have you got there, I say?"

"O father, the pig, the pig, do come and taste how nice the burnt pig eats."

The ears of Ho-ti tingled with horror. He cursed his son, and he cursed that ever he should beget a son that sould eat burnt pig.

Bo-bo, whose scent was wonderfully sharpened since morning, soon raked out another pig, and fairly rending it asunder, thrust the lesser half by main force into the fists of Ho-ti, still shouting out, "Eat, eat, eat the burnt pig, father, only taste – O Lord!" – with such-like barbarous ejaculations, cramming all the while as if he would choke.

Ho-ti trembled every joint while he grasped the abominable thing, wavering whether he should not put his son to death for an unnatural young monster, when the crackling scorching his fingers, as it had done his son's, and applying the same remedy to them, he in his turn tasted some of its flavour, which, make what sour mouths he would for a pretence, proved not altogether displeasing to him. In conclusion (for the manuscript here is a little tedious), both father and son fairly sat down to the mess, and never left off till they had dispatched all that remained of the litter.

Bo-bo was strictly enjoined not to let the secret escape, for the neighbors would certainly have stoned them for a couple of abominable wretches, who could think of improving upon the good meat which God had sent them. Nevertheless, strange stories got about. It was observed that Ho-ti's cottage burnt down now more frequently than ever. Nothing but fires from this time forward. Some would break out in broad day, others in the night-time. As often as the sow farrowed, so sure was the house of Ho-ti to be in a blaze; and Ho-ti himself, which was the most remarkable, instead of chastising his son, seemed to grow more indulgent to him than ever. At length they were watched, the terrible mystery discovered, and father and son summoned to take their trial at Pekin, then an inconsiderable assize town. Evidence was given, the obnoxious food itself produced in court, and verdict about to be pronounced, when the foreman of the jury begged that some of the burnt pig, of which the culprits stood accused, might be handed into the box. He handled it, and they all handled it, and burning their fingers, as Bo-bo and his father had done before them, and nature prompting to each of them the same remedy, against the face of all the facts, and the clearest charge which judge had ever given, – to the surprise of the whole court, townsfolk, strangers, reporters, and all present – without leaving the box, or any manner of consultation whatever, they brought in a simultaneous verdict of Not Guilty.

The judge, who was a shrewd fellow, winked at the manifest iniquity of the decision: and, when the court was dismissed, went privily, and bought up all the pigs that could be had for love or money. In a few days his lordship's town-house was observed to be on fire. The thing took wing, and now there was nothing to be seen but fires in every direction. Fuel and pigs grew enormously dear all over the district. The insurance offices one and all shut up shop. People built slighter and slighter every day, until it was feared that the very science of architecture would in no long time be lost to the world. Thus this custom of firing houses continued, till in process of time, says my manuscript, a sage arose, like our Locke, who made a discovery that the flesh of a swine, or indeed of any other animal, might be cooked (*burnt*, as they called it) without the necessity of consuming a whole house to dress it. Then first began the rude form of a gridiron. Roasting by the string, or spit, came in a century or two later, I forget in whose dynasty. By such slow degrees, concludes the manuscript, do the most useful, and seemingly the most obvious arts, make their way among mankind. —

Without placing too implicit faith in the account above given, it must be agreed, that if a worthy pretext for so dangerous an experiment as setting houses on fire (especially in these days) could be assigned in favour of any culinary object, that pretext and excuse might be found in roast pig.

Of all the delicacies in the whole *mundus edibilis*, I will maintain it to be the most delicate – *princeps obsoniorum.*

I speak not of your grown porkers – things between pig and pork – those hobbydehoys – but a young and tender suckling – under a moon old – guiltless as yet of the sty – with no original speck of the *amor immunditiæ*, the hereditary failing of the first parent, yet manifest – his voice as yet not broken, but something between a childish treble and a grumble – the mild forerunner, or *præludium*, of a grunt.

He must be roasted. I am not ignorant that our ancestors ate them seethed, or boiled – but what a sacrifice of the exterior tegument!

There is no flavour comparable, I will contend, to that of the crisp, tawny, well-watched, not over-roasted, *crackling*, as it is well called – the very teeth are invited to their share of the pleasure at this banquet in overcoming the coy, brittle resistance – with the adhesive oleaginous – O call it not fat! But as indefinable sweetness growing up to it – the tender blossoming of fat – fat cropped in the bud – taken in the shoot – in the first innocence – the cream and quintessence of the child-pig's yet pure food – the lean, no lean, but a kind of animal manna – or, rather, fat and lean (if it must be so) so blended and running into each other, that both together make but one ambrosian result, or common substance.

Behold him, while he is "doing" – it seemeth rather a refreshing warmth, than a scorching heat, that he is so passive to. How equably he twirleth round the string! – Now he is just done. To see the extreme sensibility of that tender age, he hath wept out his pretty eyes – radiant jellies – shooting stars.

See him in the dish, his second cradle, how meek he lieth! – wouldst thou have had this innocent grow up to the grossness and indocility which too often accompany maturer swinehood? Ten to one he would have proved a glutton, a sloven, an obstinate, disagreeable animal – wallowing in all manner of filthy conversation – from these sins he is happily snatched away –

Ere sin could blight, or sorrow fade,
Death came with timely care –

his memory is odoriferous – no clown curseth, while his stomach half rejecteth, the rank bacon – no coal-heaver bolteth him in reeking sausages – he hath a fair sepulchre in the grateful stomach of the judicious epicure – and for such a tomb might be content to die.

He is the best of Sapors. Pine-apple is great. She is indeed almost too transcendent – a delight, if not sinful, yet so like to sinning, that really a tender-conscienced person would do well to pause – too ravishing for mortal taste, she woundeth and excoriateth the lips that approach her –

like lovers' kisses, she biteth – she is a pleasure bordering on pain from the fierceness and insanity of her relish – but she stoppeth at the palate – she meddleth not with the appetite – and the coarsest hunger might barter her consistently for a mutton-chop.

Pig – let me speak his praise – is no less provocative of the appetite, than he is satisfactory to the criticalness of the censorious palate. The strong man may batten on him, and the weakling refuseth not his mild juices.

Unlike to mankind's mixed characters, a bundle of virtues and vices, inexplicably intertwisted, and not to be unraveled without hazard, he is – good throughout. No part of him is better or worse than another. He helpeth, as far as his little means extend, all around. He is the least envious of banquets. He is all neighbours' fare.

I am one of those, who freely and grudgingly impart a share of the good things of this life which fall to their lot (few as mine are in this kind) to a friend. I protest I take as great an interest in my friend's pleasures, his relishes, and proper satisfactions, as in mine own. "Presents," I often say, "endear Absents." Hares, pheasants, partridges, snipes, barn-door chickens (those "tame villatic fowl"), capons, plovers, brawn, barrels of oysters, I dispense as freely as I receive them. I love to taste them, as it were, upon the tongue of my friend. But a stop must be put somewhere. One would not, like Lear, "give everything." I make my stand upon pig. Methinks it is an ingratitude to the Giver of all good flavours, to extradomiciliate, or send out of the house, slightingly, (under pretext of friendship, or I know not what) a blessing so particularly adapted, predestined, I may say, to my individual palate – It argues an insensibility.

I remember a touch of conscience in this kind of school. My good old aunt, who never parted from me at the end of a holiday without stuffing a sweet-meat, or some nice thing, into my pocket, had dismissed me one evening with a smoking plum-cake, fresh from the oven. In my way to school (it was over London Bridge) a grey-headed old beggar saluted me (I have no doubt at this time of day he was a counterfeit). I had no pence to console him with, and in the vanity of self-denial, and the very coxcombry of charity, school-boy-like, I made him a present of – the whole cake! I walked on a little, buoyed up, as one is on such occasions, with a sweet soothing of self-satisfaction; but, before I had got to the end of the bridge, my better feelings returned, and I burst into tears, thinking how ungrateful I had been to my good aunt, to go and give her good gift away to a stranger, that I had never seen before, and who might be a bad man for aught I knew; and then I thought of the pleasure my aunt would be taking in thinking that I – I myself, and not another –

would eat her nice cake – and what should I say to her the next time I saw her – how naughty I was to part with her pretty present – and the odour of that spicy cake came back upon my recollection, and the pleasure and the curiosity I had taken in seeing her make it, and her joy when she sent it to the oven, and how disappointed she would feel that I had never had a bit of it in my mouth at last – and I blamed my impertinent spirit of alms-giving, and out-of-place hypocrisy of goodness – and above all I wished never to see the face again of that insidious, good-for-nothing, old grey imposter.

Our ancestors were nice in their method of sacrificing these tender victims. We read of pigs whipt to death with something of a shock, as we hear of any other obsolete custom. The age of discipline is gone by, or it would be curious to inquire (in a philosophical light merely) what effect this process might have towards intenerating and dulcifying a substance, naturally so mild and dulcet as the flesh of young pigs. It looks like refining a violet. Yet we should be cautious, while we condemn the inhumanity, how we censure the wisdom of the practice. It might impart a gusto –

I remember an hypothesis, argued upon by the young students, when I was at St. Omer's, and maintained with much learning and pleasantry on both sides, "Whether, supposing that the flavour of a pig who obtained his death by whipping *(per flagellationem extremam)* superadded a pleasure upon a palate of a man more intense than any possible suffering we can conceive in the animal, is man justified in using that method of putting an animal to death?" I forget the decision.

His sauce should be considered. Decidedly, a few bread crumbs, done up with his liver and brains, and a dash of mild sage. But, banish, dear Mrs. Cook, I beseech you, the whole onion tribe. Barbecue your whole hogs to your palate, steep them in shalots, stuff them out with plantations of the rank and guilty garlic; you cannot poison them, or make them stronger than they are – but consider, he is weakling – a flower.

Introduction to the Second Edition

The central theme of this book is to present a factual account, with suitable interpretation from someone who has been intimately involved in most aspects of both pig science and production for many years, of the development of pig breeds and husbandry methods over the last millennium in the UK, although the last two centuries have received most attention. It is therefore perhaps not 'history' as would be defined by professional historians, but a rather more earthy treatise drawing on a wide range of contemporary agricultural texts.

It is interesting to note how popular pig breed history has become. Devotees of modern named breeds are keen to establish a lengthy genealogy as a means, somehow, of confirming the quality of that breed. The further back the better. Humans have always been obsessed with family trees (again, the further back the better) and now the pig is receiving attention. The first edition of this book attempted to point out in some considerable detail that such an approach with pigs was not valid (and, on reflection, it is also not much use as an indicator of quality in humans).

Tracing the historical development of different named breeds is undoubtedly a fascinating but complicated area of study. Although the introduction of herd books towards the end of the nineteenth century made the task easier (as long as the herd books were themselves accurate descriptors of lineage – a matter for considerable debate), the late eighteenth and early nineteenth centuries are much more interesting. However, there is considerably less information available for this earlier period. Accordingly, there has to be an almost complete reliance on contemporary agricultural texts supplemented by study of surviving paintings and lithographs.

The chief basis for the study of breed history is the name of the breed itself, with modern authors using each and every historical reference to a specific breed as evidence for its existence in the form in which it is currently known. This approach, however, has no role in tracing breed development for reasons which are contained within the historical record itself and become apparent only when those involved in the subject critically review references.

Pigs readily interbreed, giving rise to a variety of shapes and colours, of which the Victorian paintings of Herring (both senior and junior) of various farmyard scenes are an eloquent demonstration. They range from almost completely black to virtually all white with various intermediate forms (spotted, sheeted). The Herrings' paintings are in all likelihood accurate descriptions of the average farm, and they demonstrate absolutely no uniformity of colour, shape or form. The notion that there were named breeds with fixed characteristics is therefore highly unlikely.

In fact, the most likely basis for breed nomenclature was simply the geographical area in which the pig was found. This should never be used to suggest that there was, nationally, a specific breed type with a particular name. There is extensive coverage given to this question in the book, but it might be worthwhile providing more information in this introduction to support this opinion.

Take as an example the Sussex pig. Many descriptions were applied to it. Thus Youatt in 1847 described it as being 'white at one extremity, black at the other', while Sydney in 1860 considered (while commenting upon the confusion between the Essex and the Sussex) that the Sussex was entirely black and had been used by Lord Western to turn the old sheeted Essex black.

Youatt himself had attempted to trace pig breed development, but had to conclude that 'the actual stock from which some of the present choicest races of swine sprang cannot be traced farther back than some ancestor or ancestress celebrated for the number of prizes he or she or their immediate descendants have won'.

A cursory examination of prize lists for the Royal Show is most revealing. Taking 1842 as an example (Youatt would have been familiar with this year), the list of breeders and 'breeds' is indeed lengthy (at a time when prizes were awarded merely for best boar, reserve best boar, best sow and best pen of three breeding sow pigs). There are many references to 'breeds' which have familiar names (Improved Essex, Berkshire) but there is a distinct impression that most breed names identify geographical origin rather than a specific breed type.

In 1842 William Pearce of Chippenham, Wiltshire, had a Wiltshire/Berkshire boar (Chippenham is not far from the boundary of these two counties), and Capt. Lewis Shedden had a Surrey and Berkshire (with one cross of Sussex) boar – this was probably a widely-travelled animal and it was only nine months old.

The probability of the geographical location as a basis for naming a pig is reinforced with other examples: William Ellison from Sizergh Castel near Kendal had a 10½-month-old Sizergh boar, Thomas Goodlake of Wadley House near Faringdon Berkshire showed a Wadley boar, and the Rt Hon Charles Shaw Lefevre MP from Heckfield, Hertfordshire, had a boar of the – yes – Heckfield breed (although it was admitted that it was only three-quarters Heckfield with a bit of a Berkshire cross). Sometimes pigs were named after their owners – the Rev John Vane had a boar of his own breed, bred by himself.

I note that there is no rush amongst modern pig 'historians' to identify the current status of the Sizergh, Wadley, Heckfield and Vane 'breed' of pigs.

The confusion over nomenclature and appearance is not confined to textual references. Pictorial descriptions of pigs, other than those by artists such as the Herrings who were only interested in depicting typical farmyard scenes, must be viewed cautiously. Livestock portraits were frequently commissioned by proud owners keen to portray their animals in the best possible light. If a particular shape or form was regarded as 'perfect' (many animals were described as such!) then the picture would duly conform to this idealised structure. On the other hand, written descriptions underneath paintings are often very informative. As an example, the two prints in Mavor's text of 1809 are quite dissimilar even though both are described as Berkshires and both come from that county (see p. 36). More worrying is that the animal owned by Loveden (the lower pig on p. 36) was described subsequently by Loudon (admittedly a few years later in 1831) as Chinese, illustrating the importance of cross-referencing in any historical analysis. There are other examples. Pitt's text on Staffordshire from 1796 (see p. 17) includes two animals, both described as Staffordshire boars. The former was referred to as the 'Prickear mixed' and the latter as 'Berkshire mixed' by Dickson no more than ten years later. Pitt's Staffordshire sow and pigs were called Berkshires by Loudon. The preponderance of spotted, blotched and sheeted animals (to say nothing of the variation in shape) points rather more to a complete lack of breeding policy ('pigs into the melting pot', as Trow-Smith remarked).

Such confusion was certainly not confined to the eighteenth and nineteenth centuries. Loudon's Hampshire was referred to as an Old English Berkshire by Layley and Malden a hundred years later in 1935, and the problem persists. A portrait sold in 1986 of perhaps the biggest pig ever seen in the UK (although this is a matter for debate) was purportedly a Gloucester Old Spot. The animal was dispatched in 1774 (Culley, in 1807, provided graphic details), but the attributed artist (again a matter for debate) did not undertake the work until some fifty years later. Its appearance bears more resemblance to Low's Berkshire (not that this name is of any help) which, intriguingly, was painted at around the same time (1840s) and 'Midland Plum Pudding' (a description used fairly widely in the early nineteenth century) would be better as a generic description of one sort of animal found!

Moving forward, there have been major developments in both the pig industry and the role of minority breeds in the UK over the last fifteen years. Both are considered below in the Postscript.

Finally, it was never my intention to provide a commentary on matters artistic and allegorical. The pig appears throughout history, art, literature and general matters cultural; this has been the subject of many authoritative and thoroughly readable texts which really cannot be bettered, including *Farm Animal Portraits* (1996); *The Ubiquitous Pig* (1992); *Pigs – A Troughful of Treasures* (1981); *The Symbolic Pig* (1961); and *The Hog Book* (1978). Those seeking sentimental coverage of the pig (the dreadful 'Miss Piggy', the appalling 'Babe', the ridiculous 'Tamworth Two') will be disappointed. They are advised to look elsewhere for their unusual and transient pleasures.

The main object of this book is to deal with the really important features of the relationship between pigs and humans. It is essentially a eulogy on the animal's contribution to our sustenance (not always successfully, but that is not the pig's fault), not an analysis of how entertaining or appealing the pig might be. And there will be no descriptions of the relative intelligence of pigs, which seems to be a preoccupation of many. When asked how clever is the pig, the only sensible answer is that it is cleverer, far cleverer, than humans at being a pig. Or, as a French postcard remarked: 'L'homme se croit très fin, mais pour chercher les truffes, il ne vaut pas le dernier des cochons.'

Introduction to the First Edition

Throughout history the domestic pig has been sadly and unjustly neglected, while its more illustrious cousin the wild boar has, since classical times, been revered by warriors, hunters and composers of epic poems. The fourth labour of Hercules was to capture the Erymanthian boar, and the young Odysseus was permanently scarred while hunting. The ferocity of the boar during the chase was chronicled in Celtic and Scandinavian tales, and the Anglo-Saxons relished the challenge of pursuing the beast. Hunting wild boar was the pursuit of the nobility and, in medieval Europe, was considered one of the most taxing and courageous of activities.

Although the domestic pig was the major source of meat for the population from Roman times, if not earlier, until well after the Conquest, its reputation has never been good. Derogatory comments are scattered throughout literature, but for sheer abuse, it is hard to equal the following passage:

> Of all the quadrupeds that we know, or at least certainly of all those that come under the husbandman's care, the Hog appears to be the foulest, the most brutish, and the most apt to commit waste wherever it goes. The defects of its figure seem to influence its dispositions: all its ways are gross, all its inclinations are filthy, and all its sensations concentrate in a furious lust, and so eager a gluttony, that it devours indiscriminately whatever comes in its way.

John Mills, the author of this passage, felt so strongly on the subject that he added this at the end of a book devoted to cattle. He did accept, however, that the pig was one of the most profitable animals that a countryman could rear.

The pig's relative unpopularity – at least if opinions contained within books are to be believed – may have been a consequence of the damage it could do to crops (although this was nothing new), but was also due to the rise in importance of the sheep as a farm animal. Sheep walks were often established by clearing forests (which were the traditional fattening domain of the pig) and, not infrequently, removing the peasantry who relied upon the pig as a source of meat. Here is a possible clue, outlined by Mills, as to the pig's position. It was always a widely distributed animal, but mainly among the lower classes of the population not given to writing agricultural text books. Further evidence of its position was to be found during the pioneer animal-breeding programmes of the eighteenth and nineteenth centuries. These concentrated on the systematic improvement of breeds of cattle and sheep, but the pig remained relatively untouched until quite late, although Bakewell himself had dabbled, apparently unsuccessfully, in pig breeding. Even when attention was focused on the pig, appearance, and the production of excessive quantities of fat, were considered more important than economic advantages. The result was an animal which grunted along to the showground, was the subject of much discussion among the judges and assembled gentry, but was useless as a provider of wholesome meat for the rest of the population.

This was a sorry state for an animal that had been domesticated as early as the late neolithic or early bronze age. The pig had followed the dog and sheep into service at a time when permanent settlements practising agriculture were established. Pigs are not easy animals to herd, and nomadic cultures have therefore usually not bothered with them. Ironically it has been suggested by Zeuner that the pig was domesticated because, as a wild animal, it caused considerable damage to the crops of these early settlers. Thus, on the assumption that prevention is better than cure, the animal was brought under a degree of control, and the uneasy relationship that has continued ever since was begun.

Domestication was not confined to a single location, and was probably of the local wild types. The wild pig of Europe is *Sus scrofa*, and *S. vittatus* is one example of the pigs that originated from South East Asia. Several other minor species have been identified, and this, coupled with the fact that pigs readily interbreed, makes any attempt at classification difficult. Early European sites have, confusingly, produced remains of more than one type, both a domestic version of *S. scrofa* and a smaller apparently more popular type, referred to as *S. scrofa pallustris*, or the early domestic (turbary) pig. This animal bears a similarity to the Eastern pig and from information reviewed by

Zeuner is sometimes assumed to have been descended from it. However, the difficulty of transporting pigs several thousand miles would have been great, and it was not until the late eighteenth century that *S. vittatus* made any major impact on the British pig. The most likely inference is that the turbary pig was descended from the small wild pig of South Eastern Europe.

In classical times the turbary pig was, by all accounts, a long-legged, razor-backed, dark brown and bristly animal, to all intents and purposes the same as the domestic pig found in Britain during Anglo-Saxon times. This seems an appropriate point from which to begin a description of the development of pig breeds in Britain.

Acknowledgments

I would like to thank the staff of the Library at the School of Agriculture, Nottingham University, for considerable help in locating obscure references and for access to the rare books section; Mike Potter of the Meat and Livestock Commission, Bletchley, for advice, statistics and many of the photographs of modern breeds and of Buffon's orchard pig; Dr Richard Colyer, Institute of Rural Sciences, University College of Wales, Aberystwyth, for the loan of Mills' *A Treatise on Cattle* and *Dictionarium Rusticum*; the Rare Breeds Survival Trust, Stoneleigh, Warwickshire, for information on modern minority breeds of pigs; the National Pig Breeders Association, Watford, Herts, for information on pure breeds of pigs; and Carol Stanton for deciphering the original manuscript.

1

The Anglo-Saxon and Medieval Pig

We have seen that the dominant type in Anglo-Saxon and medieval Europe was most likely the primitive prick-eared pig, and it is unlikely that any attempt was made to improve it. However, this was perhaps due less to a lack of interest in improvement *per se* than to the conditions under which the vast majority of pigs were kept. Thus a consideration of pig husbandry and management is integral to an understanding of the existence of breed types.

The foraging and grubbing activities of the pig can be fairly destructive to pastures, and although herbage provided a fair proportion of the food required by the pig during the spring, summer and early autumn, in Anglo-Saxon England access to pasture was normally restricted to animals which had been ringed or yoked in an effort to curb these activities. Even access to corn stubble after harvest was frequently dependent upon the same conditions.

This illustration from the eleventh-century Cotton Manuscript shows pigs being driven into the forest to consume acorns in the autumn (British Library).

Most references to the keeping of pigs during this time describe the invaluable role played by the vast forests, which surrounded the outlying pastures of most villages, as a source of food for the pig, particularly during autumn and winter. The predominant sorts of food eaten were acorns and beech nuts (often referred to as mast).

These, supplemented with berries and roots, particularly of bracken, provided an ideal diet for fattening. Thus the greatest concentration of pigs were associated with the larger tracts of forests, rather than the predominantly arable holdings, although they tended to be found everywhere. Spencer cites a law of King Ine (A.D. 640) which imposed penalties for burning mast-producing trees, and fixed the value of a tree by the number of swine that could find shelter under it. In Domesday book, woods tended to be classified according to their pig-holding capacity; presumably the better ones were those containing the largest proportion of oak and beech trees. Despite the restrictions mentioned above, the need to feed large numbers of pigs before acorns and mast were ripe presupposes that areas of common pasture must have been set aside for this purpose, although there is apparently little evidence for this.

The right to allow pigs to forage in the woods during the autumn (known as denbera in Anglo-Saxon England, and as pannage under the Normans) was a valuable privilege. It had to be paid for either in kind (i.e. a certain proportion of the pigs slaughtered) or as direct cash payments (which gradually became more common). Thus under Alfred the payment varied according to the size of the animal: at the end of the season one third of those pigs with three fingers of fat, one quarter of those with two fingers, and one fifth of those with a thumb were due as payment. By the reign of Henry VIII the payment was 1*d* or 1½*d* per head for a much shorter season. Payment for pannage was governed by strict codes, and was usually paid to the feudal lord or estate owner at the start of the season. Payment was often obligatory even if the right was not taken up. Failure to pay, usually by Michaelmas (29 September) was severely punished, frequently by a refusal of permission to sell the animals – this would have been particularly damaging to the owner as food supplies dwindled with the onset of winter. Revenue from pannage could be considerable, and was often more than that received from sales of wood and charcoal from the forest.

In addition to exacting payment for the right of pannage, the feudal lords or estate owners also limited the length of the season, since they recognised the damage that could be caused to woodland

The seasonality of pig production, particularly during medieval times, was often the subject of manuscript illustrations. Slaughter scenes like this one from the early fourteenth-century Queen Mary's Psalter were particularly common during late autumn when food was becoming scarce (British Library).

(principally saplings and tree roots) by foraging pigs. The opening of the pannage season was announced officially and, traditionally, in Anglo-Saxon England it began on 29 August and extended up until 31 December. The importance and universality of this method of fattening can be gauged from a study of manuscripts and other documents of the time. Frequently calendars depict the driving of swine to forests where they are seen to consume nuts, and this is particularly associated with the month of October.

The day-to-day management of pigs was traditionally in the hands of the village swineherds, who collected animals from households in the morning and tended them during the day, often in very large groups. In fact the size of these herds was such that it has been suggested that the swineherds would have been unable to keep an eye on all the pigs, and that only the weaker, smaller and heavily pregnant animals received any attention – the remainder being allowed to roam in a semi-wild state until needed. But swineherds were legally responsible for all the animals in their charge, and there are many records of fines imposed for damage done by pigs. Swineherds frequently remained with their pigs during the night, sharing rudely constructed shelters with them (it was appreciated that pigs required relatively dry and warm sleeping quarters).

It has been claimed by Laurans that there is no evidence as to whether the swineherds were the owners or the keepers of these large herds; there appear to be no records of the number of pigs owned by an individual. Tributary tenants, whose herds were supplied by the manor and reverted back on the swineherd's death, were becoming common in the ninth century. The pig was the poor man's animal, and records only tell us the number of animals per parish or manor.

It is known, however, that the swineherds received payment for their services, usually in kind. For example, in the twelfth century in Glastonbury a swineherd's payment was as follows:

1. One sucking pig per year
2. The entrails of the best pig slaughtered
3. The tails of all pigs slaughtered (pig tail soup being regarded as something of a delicacy)

and in Basingstoke in 1389:

1. $\frac{1}{2}$d per quarter per pig
2. $\frac{1}{2}$d per quarter per 2 litter pigs
3. An annual dinner from each tenant

– an example of how direct cash payments were gradually replacing payment in kind.

Because of the lack of winter food, many animals were killed and salted down in early winter. The age of slaughter is difficult to determine. Trow-Smith has claimed that the Anglo-Saxon pig took three years to reach maturity, while other sources, cited by Laurans (although admittedly referring to later dates), mention slaughter ages during the later Middle Ages of between 18 and 24 months. Thus pigs were well into their second year, at least, at slaughter, which raises the problem of how they were wintered during their first (bearing in mind the acute shortages of food usual at this time of year). A possible answer is provided by records from medieval France relating to the length of the pannage season, which was occasionally extended up to the appearance of the first leaves of spring or even as far as St George's Day (23 April). Walter of Henley acknowledged that pigs would need extra fodder from February to April.

In addition to large herds of semi-domestic pigs, there were true wild boars in the forest, hunted by the Anglo-Saxons often to such an extent that they suffered a serious decline in numbers. A law of

William I decreed that anyone found guilty of hunting a wild boar should have his eyes put out. Whether this was a genuine attempt at conservation, or a means of restricting hunting to the nobility, is a matter for speculation.

However, even if the domestic pig represented an improvement over the wild boar – and there is no evidence to suggest that there was a great deal of difference between the two other than the smaller size of the former – the practice of driving pigs into the woodlands during the autumn and winter to forage for food must have required a particularly hardy animal. Moreover, with such large herds and extensive conditions, mating must have been mainly uncontrollable, even, possibly, to the extent of cross-breeding with true wild types, and thus little selective breeding could have been practised. It seems that improvement was both unwanted and impractical. On the other hand, it was fairly common practice in medieval France for the boar to be the property of the feudal lord or church, and payment would be duly charged for his services. This could be interpreted as a means of raising further revenue rather than as an attempt at a breeding policy. Matings were certainly fairly indiscriminate in terms of time (from the evidence of well-defined categories of levies imposed for pannage according to age), although the aim was usually to farrow down in the spring. However, it is also claimed that sows tended to be culled after their third litter, and that pigs from this litter were most sought after as replacements, only the best and healthiest pigs being selected (apparently white ones were preferred). This is not necessarily evidence for an improvement in stock, and may simply have been a means of avoiding weaker animals.

The pig played a major part in medieval agricultural systems, and it has been suggested that pig-keeping was one of the most important rural occupations: it probably supplied one of the countryside's chief products. Revenue from keeping pigs was often considerable, and pigmeat, their most important product, was well suited to preservation, in contrast to beef and mutton which became tough and dry on salting. The pig was important as a source of essential fat in an age when the extraction of vegetable oils was difficult. Pigs could be easily reared on poor quality land. Pig-keeping from Saxon times until the twelfth and thirteenth centuries represented a good example of adaptation to a natural environment. At a time when food resources were scarce, pigs were a source of first-class nutritional products which did not compete with man for food – being reared and fattened primarily on grass and woodland.

Thus the pig was a source of revenue, provided a secure form of winter food, and made a significant contribution towards a balanced diet. Laurans has claimed that its role as a major contributor to the development of medieval society has rarely been acknowledged.

Medieval manuscripts often refer to the importance of forests in providing food for fattening pigs in the autumn. In this illustration from Queen Mary's Psalter swineherds are knocking acorns from the trees for consumption by pigs. This is also a useful pictorial guide to the appearance of pigs at the time. They were evidently small, long-legged, razor-backed, bristly and ruddy-brown with prick ears (British Library)

2

Medieval Decline and Changes in Husbandry

The causes of decline

The pig reached a peak in terms of its agricultural importance in Britain sometime around the Conquest, but its decline was somewhat later in France, probably at about the end of the twelfth century. There are two main reasons for this fall in popularity: the restriction of pannage and the rise in importance of sheep.

The value of woods apart from their role in providing food for pigs had always been recognised. Restrictions in the length of the pannage season, and the fact that there were often laws against knocking acorns and mast off trees with sticks because of the possible damage that such a practice might do, are evidence of this. However, the value of wood and charcoal began to increase gradually during the twelfth century, and consequently the damage caused by the activities of foraging pigs (mainly to saplings) became progressively more serious economically. This was reflected in a gradual reduction in the traditional time allowed for pannage. From the Conquest to the mid-fourteenth century access to woodland was restricted to between six and eight weeks during October and November (although a charter of Henry III in 1225, presumably referring to royal forests, only allowed pannage from Midsummer to Michaelmas). During the reign of Henry VIII, the official pannage season extended from Michaelmas to Martinmas (29 September to 11 November), and swine in mid-sixteenth-century Lancashire were allowed to roam from the end of August to sowing time, provided that they were properly ringed and did no harm, in default of which a fine of 4*d* was imposed. These limitations can be contrasted with the traditional pannage season of four months or more during Anglo-Saxon times. There was also a gradual erosion of forests to make more land available for arable crops, particularly in response to an increasing population in the thirteenth century, which reduced the area of woodland available for foraging. Later population decline, caused by the Black Death, did not necessarily have the reverse effect. In fact acute labour shortages coupled with the rise in importance of sheep meant that more holdings were laid down to grass. Wool production was both more profitable and far less labour intensive.

Thus the decline of importance of the pig may also have been due partly to the considerable increase in demand, both at home and abroad, for English wool, which was considered to be of the finest quality. This trend discriminated against the pig, although its effects may not have been a major factor in the pig's decline, since in 1327 in England, a two-year-old pig was worth twice as much as a fat sheep with fleece.

Changes in pig husbandry

Increased difficulty in obtaining traditional sources of food was the major reason why large-scale pig production declined during the Middle Ages. The alternatives to grazing, acorns, beech mast and all the other products of the forest, were cereals and pulses. Occasionally these were used to feed pigs, but there was still virtually complete reliance on pannage for fattening, so much so that treeless manors rarely recorded any swine in the early thirteenth century, or only those numbers that could exist on stubbles and other waste. Cereals and pulses were expensive, and by consuming them the pig was competing directly with man. Thus one of its major attributes – its ability to consume and thrive on foodstuffs of little use to man or other livestock species – was not being exploited. The consequences of harvest failure were now doubly serious as there was an increasing reliance on arable crops (themselves possibly declining in overall output due to the move towards pasture) to feed both animals and man, and dwindling use was made of the wild products traditionally eaten by pigs. On a very localised basis, however, pigs were sometimes fed on specialised by-products such as whey or brewers' grains.

A major consequence of these developments was that the pig and its role in the community gradually changed. The hardy semi-wild pig of the open forest rooting around for a wide range of food now tended to be housed for longer periods, usually on a 'one per household' basis, and fed predominantly on kitchen waste. It can be argued that this change in pig-keeping was of paramount importance in the development of types of pig that were less able to withstand the harsh conditions of the open forest and more suited to an indoor existence. It is quite likely that the move towards improvement of types away from the semi-wild originated at this time, even though, overall, the pig was declining in importance.

Because of the pig's omnivorous habits the new diet was still regarded as perfectly adequate. In fact the pig's ability to consume and thrive upon almost anything was considered a positive virtue, and the pig of the seventeenth century has been described by Markham as:

> the husbandman's best scavenger and the housewife's most wholesome sink ... for his food and his living is by that which would else rot in the yard and make it beastly.

Similarly pigs kept in towns were frequently allowed to scavenge for food during the day. Coates, writing in the *Pig Breeders' Annual* of 1936/7, suggested that some pigs during the sixteenth century were fattened on peas and beans, dairy and brewery wastes.

However, traditional means of pig-keeping were still practised, and must have been reasonably common in Tudor times, to judge from the advice of Thomas Tusser, a contemporary agricultural author, who suggested activities during the year which were important to ensure successful rearing. For example:

> October good blast
> To blowe the hog mast.

This indicates that beech nuts still played an important role in the feeding of pigs, and that a strong wind was important to blow them off the trees. Similarly, again referring to October:

> Though plenty of acornes, the porkling to fat,
> not taken in season, may perish by that.
> If rattling or swelling get once to the throte,
> thou loosest thy porkling, a crowne to a grote.

The virtues of acorns as a means of fattening were still recognised, although the possible dangers of feeding them out of season were obviously well understood. Advice for the month of November continued with:

> Let hog once go fat, loose nothing of that.
> When mast is gone, hog falleth anon.
> Still fat up some, till Shroftide come.
> Now porke and sous, beares tack in house.

Once all the food had been consumed pigs would deteriorate in condition. However, it was advisable to keep on some pigs until Shrove Tuesday (Shroftide). That foods other than acorns and mast were available to pigs in the forest is suggested in the following verse, also referring to November:

> Get pole, boy mine
> beate hawes to swine.
> Drive hog to the wood
> breake rootes be good.

Other verses deal with additional aspects of traditional pig-keeping. The importance of the swineherd and the possible damage caused by roaming pigs is mentioned in April's calendar:

> Get swineherd for hog,
> but kill not with dog.
> Where swineherd doth lack
> Corne goeth to wrack.

Remnants of traditional pig-bearing systems continued, in fact, well beyond Tudor times, and were recorded during the early eighteenth century by, for example, John Mortimer, who warned about the development of swellings in the neck which were sometimes a consequence of feeding acorns. In 1794 Abraham and William Driver described the feeding of the famous Hampshire hogs on acorns and beech mast principally around the forest. In the early nineteenth century the inhabitants of the New Forest had the right of pannage (or pawnage) from fifteen days before Michaelmas (29 September) to forty days after, during which time the swineherd apparently kept the pigs from straying by his musical abilities on the horn.

The *Journal of the Royal Agricultural Society** in 1843 indicated that the use of acorns beneficially hardened the meat because, it was suggested, of the presence of tannins. Moreover records show that the inhabitants of the New Forest in the mid-nineteenth century were still allowed pannage rights from 25 September to 22 November, at a cost of 1*s* and 2*s* for pigs under and over a year old respectively. This provided some considerable revenue for the Crown, as the number of pigs turned out were 19,813 between the years 1865 to 1869 inclusive, according to the *JRASE* of 1871. However, it was also mentioned that supplementary feeds were necessary, as to fatten pigs exclusively upon acorns or mast was not particularly successful. As late as 1909, John Nisbett wrote that acorns were widely used for fattening swine – Gloucestershire farmers apparently considered them superior to beans for this purpose – although a surfeit could produce a condition referred to as 'garget' (a sort of distemper, by all accounts), which also resulted from excessive consumption of beech mast. Even the seasonality of pig production was common up to the end of the nineteenth century, as was the fact that individual households frequently had one pig each for fattening. The pig in Thomas Hardy's *Jude the Obscure* had to be slaughtered one autumn day specifically because it had finished all the food set aside for it.

Although we have some evidence relating to the keeping and fattening of pigs from the Conquest to the beginning of the eighteenth century, there is an almost total absence of any description of specific breed types during this period. The true wild boar probably became extinct during the early Tudor period, and was reintroduced from Germany by Charles I. By the mid-nineteenth century (after probable crosses with the domestic pig) these swine were found only in the more thickly wooded and remoter parts of the New Forest and were rapidly becoming extinct. They were referred to as true New Forest hogs and were generally dark brindled or black with prick ears.

There is nothing to suggest that the domestic pig was far removed from the wild except in its smaller size. However, we have noted that a gradual change in pig husbandry could have acted as a stimulus to the development of improved types. Tusser, describing pig husbandry month by month, had this advice to offer for January:

---

* Referred to as *JRASE* throughout this book.

Sowes ready to farrow at this time of the yeere
are for to be made of and counted full deere.
For now is the losse of a fare of the sow
More great then the losse of two calves of thy cow.

This has been interpreted as suggesting that pigs born in January will be weaned when wash (dairy or brewery waste) is plentiful so that they will fatten to produce pork by Michaelmas (29 September) and bacon by Christmas. This is in contrast to the minimum of eighteen months required by the Anglo-Saxon pig. Thus while there would appear to be little supporting evidence, it is possible that the improvement of the semi-wild type had, by Tudor times, resulted in a pig which could be slaughtered in its first year. The importance of nutrition cannot be overlooked, however, and this apparently considerable reduction in age at slaughter may be attributable largely to the almost year-round availability of food (be it kitchen waste, dairy offal or brewery by-products) in contrast to the strictly seasonal supply of the traditional feeds used for fattening.

One of the earliest references to the presence of specific regional types of pig (by Gervase Markham in 1683) mentions that the Leicester, during Tudor times, was renowned for its ability to fatten and produce fine carcasses. But this too may have been due largely to nutritional rather than breed factors, as the fattening diet of the Midland pig apparently consisted predominantly of quality peas and beans. Moreover Marshall referred to the fact that the greatest numbers of swine found in the country were located in Leicestershire and parts of Northamptonshire in the early eighteenth century. Peas and beans were used for fattening and apparently most of the meat was dispatched to London for victualling the Navy. Although salt pork had been an important component of the diet of sailors for many years, this is one of the earliest indications that pigs were occasionally reared for a specific outlet.

The pig's ability to fatten on waste products was increasingly being put to good use on a localised but large-scale basis from the mid-eighteenth century onwards. Distillery waste was particularly popular (e.g. brewers' grains, spent wash and even dust from the barley stores), and the large breweries in Vauxhall, Battersea and Wandsworth, for example, fattened some 9000 pigs annually. According to James and Malcolm in 1784:

Formerly, that refuse was let off into the Thames. But as the exigencies of the state required, from time to time, supplies of money, the then government found it expedient to draw a revenue from that spirit. An expedient was hit upon for converting that refuse or wash into a food for fattening hogs.

Pig-fattening on this scale was particularly lucrative – so much so that it was considered to be unfair competition, presumably by those who had no access to such cheap and nutritious sources of food. Store animals, kept on swedes, mangels, old beans and refuse corn, were brought in at around fifteen months old from all over the country (although those from Berkshire and the larger white types from Yorkshire, Lincolnshire and Leicestershire were preferred) and finished over a further $4\frac{1}{2}$ to 6 months. Waste from starch manufacturers was also considered nutritious, though not as highly as brewery by-products, as it had to be supplemented with peas and beans for adequate fattening. In 1807 Young described how a Sir Richard Neave had successfully fattened his hogs on a diet including biscuit-makers' sweepings.

Dairy waste was also used extensively as a fattening diet, and pigs were regarded as an important source of profit for the well-managed dairy well into the nineteenth century. Thus twenty cows could supply sufficient waste for twelve hogs to be fattened to twenty score lbs each in 1813, ten bacon and fifteen pork pigs per annum in 1855. In fact, it was considered that such feeds were essential, as the large quantities of grain that would otherwise be required would have been likely to render pig-fattening unprofitable. Quite a thriving droving industry was established, based upon the supply of Welsh store pigs to the dairying regions of Wiltshire and Gloucestershire which then supplied the subsequent bacon, considered the best in the country, to the London meat markets. Incidentally, the profitability of Welsh store pig production was apparently dependent upon whether drovers arrived in South Wales to collect the animals, as there was little other use for them.

3

The Old English and Foreign Breeds

The Old English pig

From illustrations in medieval manuscripts, it is apparent that the domestic pig of the time was long bodied, brown/black or neutral coloured with abundant bristles located predominantly along the spine. The ears were small and erect. Although it is necessary to rely entirely upon artistic impression for this description, it can be said to be fairly accurate. The pig was an everyday sight, so portraying it should have presented the artist with little difficulty, as it would had he been obliged to rely on distant memories. Illustrations are backed up by skeletal remains, which indicate that, in addition to the points outlined above, the primitive domestic pig was much smaller than the wild boar. This point is relevant in view of recent attempts to re-breed a primitive domestic pig by crossing the modern Tamworth with a wild boar. The offspring certainly bear a resemblance to the primitive pig, but are much larger.

The pictures we have of medieval pigs are, however, in marked contrast to descriptions of the unimproved early eighteenth-century British pig. Many reports of its colour and conformation exist. It was, by all accounts, found throughout the British Isles, although in addition to describing it, contemporary authors frequently mention that it was becoming less common fairly rapidly. Thus 'those approaching the original stock are the large Lancashire, Yorkshire, Cheshire with large flop ears ... which was probably the only domestic kind found throughout the kingdom' (Thomas Rowlandson in 1850); 'the old white breed still exists in Somerset as in other Western counties' (William Marshall in 1796); 'the old pigs are large, white and long eared' (Thomas Davis in 1794); '[the Shropshire was] originally high backed and large-eared, but rarely found now' (Joseph Plymley in 1803); 'remnants of the old English

The Old English pig that was common in the eighteenth century, with characteristic lop-ears, was considerably larger than the medieval pig depicted in early manuscripts. It was rapidly approaching extinction in its pure form by the mid-nineteenth century. *Above:* from Youatt (1847); *below:* from Layley & Malden (1935), who referred to it as a Berkshire. It is possible that this name was used to describe many similar types throughout the country.

breed may be seen in the larger breeds with long ears' (George Andrews in 1853). It seems that a major feature of the Old English breed was that it possessed long lop ears. It was usually white, although references to brindled or even black types do exist, and an

Old English sheeted breed* with a large white saddle on a predominantly black background was described by Low. Youatt, discussing the original pigs of some areas of the country, described the Old Yorkshire as dirty white or yellow spotted with black, the Old Northampton as covered with white coarse hair, the Old Shropshire as dirty white, grey or drab with spots of black, the Old Cheshire as black and white, white, and blue and white, and the Old Gloucester as dirty white, and similar colours are recorded for the Old Suffolk, Lincoln and Cornwall. It seems that small differences in colour are unimportant, for the descriptions all agree that the Old English was late maturing, long-legged, lop-eared, and not a particularly profitable feeder. It was clearly declining in numbers in the late eighteenth century, becoming confined to the western part of the country, as witnessed by an agricultural analysis of Kent in 1793 which mentions, in a brief description of pigs, that 'none of the large coarse types (are found)'.

Another pig of the Old English type, this time referred to as a Staffordshire. From Pitt (1796).

The origin and emergence of this type of Old English pig, in contrast to the medieval, is still something of a mystery. It has been claimed that the prick-eared type was the only pig found in medieval north-western Europe, and that it was not far removed from the wild

* i.e. with a belt or saddle of a different colour around the girth.

Staffordshire pigs of 1796. The resemblance of these to those referred to as Berkshires is clear, and suggests that they were different only in name. Subsequently they diversified, with the Berkshire eventually becoming the well known black breed and the Staffordshire evolving into the Tamworth. From Pitt (1796).

type. In contrast, Layley and Malden claimed that there was no evidence of there ever having been such a type native to the British Isles. Evidence relating to the origins of the larger lop-eared type is sparse. The presence of such a type in Celtic Gaul has been suggested by Laurans, and references to the Old French Lop-eared and to a larger, coarser and lighter-coloured northern type exist, for example, in Layley and Malden's *Evolution of the British Pig*. Evidence for the presence of such an animal before the Late Middle Ages has been discounted by Trow-Smith, although Layley and Malden claimed that a strong big type similar to the Scandinavian pig may have been introduced by the Danes.

The prick-eared type has been referred to as the 'Iberic' and was found, allegedly until fairly recently, in Central Europe and the Mediterranean. The Modern Portuguese has been likened to this medieval type. From the available evidence, which is sparse, Trow-Smith concluded:

> that the native British pig had been of the erect eared, coarsely bristled type commonly seen in medieval illustrations; that the dark brown colour was modified to dun and then to white by relatively early importations from a now completely unknown source; that these same importations were also probably responsible for the introduction of the lop ear and the marked maternal qualities usually associated with it.

The common pig of Europe, described by Long in 1886. This may have been closely related to the type responsible for modifying the medieval into the Old English. The illustration bears a striking resemblance to a print undertaken by Landseer before 1818. From Long (1886).

The colour of the Old English was varied, but black and white were probably the most usual colours. Thomas Ward's painting of 1810 (*above*; from Manchester City Art Galleries) suggests a mottled appearance, whereas the animal in Low's book of 1842 (*below*) is saddled.

Sidney, writing earlier in 1871, had come to a similar conclusion.

In addition to the Old English pig, which existed thoughout the British Isles during the early eighteenth century, other supposedly more primitive types have also been described. Youatt, writing in 1847 and agreeing with Low's comments of a few years earlier, considered that the original breeds of this country could be subdivided into two distinct types, the Old English mentioned above and the small prick-eared dusky pigs which greatly resembled the wild boar and were confined to the northern hills and Scotland. These are not to be confused with the true wild boar, which by then was extinct in this country. They roamed in large herds and by all accounts were virtually wild. The damage they could cause to arable holdings was considerable, and they frequently took new-born lambs, although, when fattened on reasonable diets, they could produce excellent pork. However, there were examples of pigs between these two types, and according to Wilson these approached the old English more and more the further south they were found.

The motives and incentives behind the improvements to the Old English pig are difficult to define. Improvement was certainly not out of place in a country where the great livestock breeders of the eighteenth century were already developing and improving breeds of cattle, sheep and horses. Despite its position of relative unpopularity in agriculture, attention was bound to focus on the pig sooner or later.

The major failing of the Old English pig was the time it took to reach maturity, when it would start laying down fat. Not only was this rarely under two years, thus requiring an expensive store period before the finishing phase, but the large body thus produced was also a handicap because the proportion of bone was high. The advantages to be gained from the use of an earlier maturing lighter-framed animal were therefore considerable. As one would expect, these improvements to existing breed types were a gradual and continuing process. Even as late as 1847 Youatt could write:

> a systematic alteration is extending itself throughout all our English breeds of swine; the large, heavy, coarse breeds are almost extinct, and a smaller race of animals – most apt to fatten, less expensive to keep, attaining earlier to maturity, and furnishing a far more delicious and delicate meat – have taken their place.

The increasing quantities of root crops, brassicas and cereals being grown for stock feed also required an earlier fattening animal, and the gradual reduction in the more extensive methods of pig production meant that hardiness was no longer of such importance. It is also possible that natural curiosity amongst farmers, coupled with an increasing opportunity to experiment with the exotic breeds that were becoming available from a rapidly expanding Empire, was an important factor.

Whatever the reasons, pig keeping from the mid-eighteenth century onwards became progressively more concerned with the development of as many new types as possible – each owner striving towards the production of the ideal pig (although this appears never to have been defined, being somewhat of a subjective notion) using whatever specimens were available. Pigs readily interbreed and have a high reproductive rate. They can therefore be moulded easily into innumerable shapes and colours by breeders with various original types at their disposal.

Foreign breeds

Numerous importations of foreign breeds now took place. This was nothing new. The Romans may well have introduced some new blood during their occupation, and the forerunner of the Old English must have arrived from somewhere, possibly as a result of agricultural contacts with the Low Countries and Scandinavia, which had its indigenous or 'Landrace' pig. However, with the lack of appreciable evidence to the contrary, it is generally assumed that the great influx of foreign breeds started around the middle of the eighteenth century, although Trow-Smith considered that a few importations before this were quite likely, and Sydney thought that overseas pigs must have been imported long before serious consideration was given to improving the pig in this country.

Of these exotic breeds, it was probably the Chinese that was to have the greatest influence on breeding. Three distinct sub-varieties of Chinese were generally recognised (white, black and tawny), although a possible seven were mentioned by Wilson, who also stated, conveniently, that all Chinese pigs could be classified as one variety, having the same form, but diversity of colour. Sydney, writing in 1871, admitted that, because China was so large, the diversity of breeds must have been considerable, although he does

The Chinese pig. From Wilson in (1849).

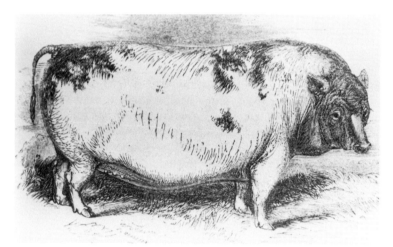

This Chinese pig, though possibly not pure, shows some of the potential for laying down fat that was to have such a devastating effect upon the native British pigs of the nineteenth century. Modern Chinese pigs show the same features. From Youatt (1847).

mention that the majority of imports to this country originated from Canton and Macao. These added qualities of fine form, quiet disposition and aptitude to fatten, to the size, adaptation, hardiness and prolificacy of the Old English, to a varying degree depending on the extent of the cross. Another, later, arrival (possibly around 1830, though maybe earlier) was the black Neapolitan, which originally

Low's Siamese pig. Although the sow was probably pure, the diversity of colour in the offspring is interesting. From Low (1842).

The Neapolitan was representative of those types found throughout the Mediterranean. From Low (1842).

came from Siam but had probably undergone a degree of interbreeding with local Italian varieties before arriving in England.

Although they were arguably the most popular, these two breeds were by no means the only arrivals. Contemporary authors mentioned other examples, including the Indo-Chinese or Siamese,

The Mediterranean, or Iberic, types were scattered throughout that region. They were common in Corsica in the 1900s (the approximate date of this postcard), and are still found in Portugal and Spain.

The Irish Greyhound was related to the Old English. What is particularly interesting about this type, apart from its ability to clear a five-barred gate with ease, is the presence of the two wattles hanging from the throat. Their function may have been to dissipate excess heat, which suggests a tropical influence. Wattles were reported as early as 1813 in the old type of pig found in Durham and, later, in the Old Gloucester. From Layley & Malden (1935)

which was black with a copper skin, a Wild Turkey pig (not to be confused with the 'tonkey' or 'tonquin' from Indo-China), a black African, a Maltese, a half African and Wild Jamaican, an Otaheitan, a German, a Barbadian and an Indian jungle pig. A breed with an entire as opposed to a cloven hoof was also recorded, as well as an unknown tropical pig whose influence on the Irish Greyhound and the Old Gloucester was to provide wattles hanging down the throat – probably used to dissipate excess body heat in the tropics. To add further confusion, Sydney mentioned that it was common to refer to all foreign breeds indiscriminately as Chinese. It is fairly safe to assume that once the early maturing qualities of the majority of these exotic breeds were realised, they were used extensively as crosses on to the Old English types.

George Garrard's pig models, from the first decade of the nineteenth century. Wild boar (*left*); Old English boar (*middle*); half-bred English and Siamese sow (*right*). British Museum (Natural History).

There are in the British Museum models of pigs produced by George Garrard in the early nineteenth century. In addition to the wild boar, they are of the Old English (with its characteristic appearance, described by many contemporary authors – although its dark colour is unlikely to have been truly representative) and 'a half-bred Siamese and English sow'. The latter specimen represents an important stage in the 'improvement' of the Old English, and is smaller, more barrel-shaped and with erect ears. With its light colour it does bear an interesting resemblance to the Middle White of later years. However, as discussed below, the diversity of form in pigs produced by innumerable crosses means that no one individual can be regarded as typical.

4

The Early Improvement of the Old English

Contemporary evidence relating to the extent of crossbreeding or 'improving' during the latter half of the eighteenth century and early nineteenth century is virtually non-existent. This makes any attempt to describe the emergence of new types rather difficult. There were no breed associations to regulate size, conformation, colour or breeding policy, which were all at the whim of the individual breeder.

The use of county, place or owners' names to describe different breeds should be treated with some caution. New breeds frequently took the name of the area or breeder associated with their development. If they were subsequently transported, it was quite possible for them to assume the name of their new owner or area, even though changes in their appearance may have been minimal. On the other hand breeders, in an attempt to promote their own breeds, occasionally named them after well established and reputable ones. Trow-Smith suggested that there was a tendency to call all large white lop-eared pigs Shropshires during the late eighteenth century, and later, once the Berkshire pig had achieved fame throughout the country, its name too was borrowed by many to describe their own pigs. Thus names alone are no guide to the existence of specific breeds.

It appears that the value of a pig was viewed mainly in terms of its particular meat-producing potential and that colour, while a moderately accurate indicator of the animal's recent ancestry and hence its fattening qualities, was only of secondary importance.

Rowlandson, in his prize-winning essay published in the *JRASE* of 1850, illustrated that, despite the apparent diversity of breed types, there were in fact only three of any real importance, and that most others were crosses of varying degree between them. The Old English contributed size of frame and prolificacy (despite the fact that a minimum of sixteen months was needed to fatten it); the advantage of the Chinese was that it could be slaughtered at around nine months or earlier; and the Neapolitan was renowned for symmetry, moderate size, flavour of meat and aptitude to fatten, as well as being an excellent mother. Davidson, writing in 1966, discounted colour as a means of classification and, like Rowlandson, arrived at three similar major types, but based on head shape. These were the concave (with a slightly dished face and pendulous lop ears covering the eyes – Celtic/Old English), the sub-concave (with an elongated head and snout, and small ears leaning forward but not flopping over the eyes – Iberian/Mediterranean/Neapolitan) and the ultra-concave (with a short, dished face and short, pricked ears – Asiatic/Chinese). He considered that the time taken to reach maturity and the production of a specific carcass type were also important. Breeders recognised the specific carcass characteristics described by Rowlandson and endeavoured to breed the ideal pig for the prevailing market conditions. Rowlandson continued by outlining some basic crosses that could be used to produce specific types. Bacon production would require a larger-framed animal, and pigs intended for this purpose would contain more of the Old English. The demand for large flitches of predominantly fat bacon was very strong, and Cobbett commented in his *Cottage Economy*:

> if a hog be more than a year old he is the better for it. Make him fat by all means. If he can walk two or three hundred yards at a time he is not well fatted. Lean bacon is the most wasteful thing that a family can use. In short it is uneatable except by drunkards who want something to stimulate their sickly appetite.

The virtues of fat as a concentrated source of dietary energy – essential for the hard physical existence of labourers – had long been recognised. In 1794 Abraham and William Driver described a pickling process in which all lean and bone was removed, and the resultant fat (which was between four and six inches thick) was salted down, after which it formed the staple diet of servants and labourers. In 1793 John Boys mentioned that the larger animals were eaten by servants rather than the gentry, who themselves preferred roasting pork produced from the smaller types. He also described how the larger hogs were frequently laid down as pickling pork in brine tubs to be fed to the ploughmen. The role of fat in the preservation of bacon by drying or salting and in rendering subsequent cooked meat more succulent was also well appreciated.

However, the appetite and taste for such meat was not universal, and there was certainly a demand for a most delicate pork or sucking pig. Rowlandson considered that such meat was best provided by pigs containing predominantly Chinese or Neapolitan (the smaller the pig required, the more of the former), and thus white pigs (suggesting a White Chinese background) were preferred for pork.

It should not be assumed, however, that an understanding of the qualities of the three major breeds, together with an appreciation of the market demands for different products, led to any orderliness in breeding policy. On the contrary, quite the reverse appears to have happened. As early as 1793, Boys remarked during his tour of Kent that 'no two pigs are the same', and John Farey, describing the pigs of Derbyshire in 1817, mentioned that they were 'a complete mixture of colour and types in this county as elsewhere'. It is hardly surprising that, given the amount of crossbreeding that was practised, the shape and colour of offspring was so diverse. Rowlandson in fact presents a most detailed description of some of his own breeding trials, one of which illustrated not only that the offspring of a white sow mated with a black Neapolitan boar were of different colours (some white, some black, some black and white, and some of a striped reddish-brown), but also that they all fattened at different rates. However, it was apparently possible judiciously to select both dam and sire from similar backgrounds and colour with a view to producing a litter that all resembled the parents, although Rowlandson implied that this was quite an unusual occurrence. Priest in 1813, reporting a litter of seven white and one black, even considered that colour marking was accidental. Due to the varied ancestry of pig types at this time, colour marking of litters as well as other characteristics must have seemed unpredictable and haphazard. As late as 1881 James Howard wrote:

apart from certain disturbing influences or causes, the male, if of pure race and descended from a stock of uniform colour, stamps the colour of the offspring.

However, he was obliged to admit in the following paragraph:

the influence of the first male is not infrequently protracted beyond the birth of the offspring of which he is the parent, and his mark is left upon subsequent progeny.

Records relating to breeding history were extremely scant, and Youatt concluded:

> each breeder of any experience has in general his own pet stock breed, frequently one that has been 'made' ... by himself or his progenitors. This will be found to be the case in all great pig-breeding localities and it frequently happens that the actual stock from which some of the present choicest races of swine sprang cannot be traced farther back than some ancestor or ancestress celebrated for the number of prizes he or she or their immediate descendants have won. At least we have found this to be the case in almost every instance in which we have endeavoured to arrive at a knowledge of the actual parent stock of some of the most perfect and valuable animals we have met with or heard of.

Thus any attempt at chronicling the development of any specific breed is beset with difficulties. Nor can the few illustrations that survive be relied upon as a guide to appearance. They were invariably commissioned by owners to show their own stock in its best light, and the bizarre appearance of some of them must have owed much to artistic licence. Nevertheless, the period up to the middle of the nineteenth century (when some of the modern breeds can be seen to emerge) is sufficiently interesting to warrant at least a consideration.

Bakewell's pig

One of the earliest recorded attempts to 'improve' a pig was made by Robert Bakewell, who was renowned more for breeding experiments with cattle and sheep. However, it is not certain whether he used exotic breeds or not. Marshall, writing in 1790, considered that Bakewell's policy was the only example of the improvement of swine by inbreeding. The effectiveness of this method was in doubt as it apparently produced pigs that were 'rickety' or 'fools'. Similarly, John Duncumb described an experiment in Hereford in 1794 in which it was accepted that Bakewell's pigs (which had been dispersed throughout the country), while being easily fattened, were defective in a number of ways. It was concluded that small animals of this sort were not of much use. Undeterred, Bakewell persisted, and the resulting pigs certainly showed signs of apparent improvement. Thus

Loudon reported in 1831 that Bakewell's pig 'has much merit' and Youatt in 1847 considered that it 'was superior in value and beauty to the old stock'. However, it is significant that Lawrence, writing much earlier in 1805, reported that it was not held in much esteem by the locals and that the undoubted foreign influence had resulted in a reduction in reproductive efficiency (in terms of small litter size), suggesting that Bakewell's pig underwent some improvement in the intervening years.

Bakewell's method involved sending the best of his sows to the same celebrated boar in the neighbourhood. Davidson has claimed that the pigs were black, suggesting a possible Neapolitan influence, but Lawrence maintained that the improved Leicester was a result of a cross between the Chinese (admittedly of unknown colour) and the Old Leicester. Wilson's description of it certainly points to a probable Chinese influence:

> its belly nearly touching the ground and its eyes and snout looking as if they were almost absorbed into the body ... yet it is somewhat tender in constitution ... and it possessed the additional disadvantage of not being so prolific as most other breeds.

Saunders Spencer alleged, in 1919, that Bakewell's pig was white, whereas Loudon claimed that the Leicester pig was light spotted. Heaton, writing in the *JRASE* of 1914, claimed that Bakewell's pig was black, but that a white improved Leicester won the gold at Smithfield in 1854. It should be pointed out that there is no evidence to suggest that the Leicester pig and Bakewell's type were synonymous. In fact they probably were not. Youatt mentioned that the Old Leicester, before Bakewell's improvement, was in fact:

> a perfect type of the original hogs of the Midland counties; large, ungainly slab-sided animals, of a light colour and spotted with brown or black.

Curiously, he added that:

> the only good parts about them were their head and ears, which showed greater traces of breeding than any other parts.

Similarly, Wilson described the Old Leicester as having 'a light spotted colour'.

To conclude this brief survey, it is worth citing Spencer who, writing at the beginning of this century, asserted that Bakewell had attempted to improve the native dark chestnut/mahogany type and had produced a rusty red/mahogany pig. This was subsequently crossed with a black boar, probably Chinese (whether by Bakewell or not is not indicated) to produce a mixture of colours including black and sandy and white! This may have been the source of the old fashioned 'plum pudding' type, common in Leicestershire, Northamptonshire and Oxfordshire early in the nineteenth century.

The Berkshire

During the mid-eighteenth century the use of clover swards as summer keep was becoming popular, and Trow-Smith argues that this contributed to the rise in popularity of the particular type of pig found in Berkshire, as it was apparently a good grazing animal. In addition, the close proximity of the London bacon markets together with the large demand for good quality store animals to be fattened on, amongst other things, the great quantities of wastes from the large London breweries (as described by James and Malcolm in 1794 in their agricultural report for Surrey) stimulated interest in the keeping of pigs. Thus Messrs Johnson at Vauxhall fattened 3000 pigs per annum on wash, grains and meal dust, Messrs Benwell of Battersea fattened between 3000 and 4000, and Bush of Wandsworth fattened 2000; the starch manufacturers quoted fattened up to 3000, but they required additional food in the form of peas and beans. Although pigs were purchased from all over the country and were thus of varying quality, most of the above specifically mentioned the Berkshire as the preferred breed. By the end of the century, the reputation of the Berkshire pig throughout the country was certainly second to none in terms of its usefulness as a store animal, its subsequent size and bacon quality, and as a cross breed on to other less improved types.

However, there is considerable confusion surrounding the appearance of the Berkshire at this time. Both Billingsley in 1798 and Marshall in 1790 mentioned a black and white Berkshire hog, and Long in 1886 considered that the original Berkshire was principally black or black and white. On the other hand, Culley in 1807 indicated that the breed was red with black spots. The presence of red to a greater or lesser degree is in fact admitted by most of the later agricultural writers. Thus Loudon in 1831 describes the Berkshire as tawny, white or reddish spotted with black; Wilson's *Rural Cyclopaedia* of 1849 described it as rufous brown, reddish or tawny white, and Low's illustration indicates a mixture of reddish brown with black spots. Spotted Berkshires were referred to in 1844 and 1852 by the *JRASE*.

According to Lawrence, writing in 1790, the original Berkshire was

> long and crooked in the snout, the muzzle turning upwards, the ears large, heavy and inclined to be pendulous, the body long and thick but not deep, the leg short, the bone large and the size very great.

Rowlandson considered that this was evidence that it must have been derived from the Old English breed. That the original Berkshire (or Old English – they must have been broadly similar) was 'improved' is unquestioned. It is difficult to determine when this happened (not least because it was in all probability a continuing process), but one possible clue is the emergence of red colourations. This may have occurred during the last half of the eighteenth century, or even earlier, as some authors consider that the original Berkshire was partially red.

Lawrence referred in 1805 to the importation of a red, or red spotted with black, breed from Barbados in the 1750s. Layley and Malden alleged that this type originally came from Spain. It was subsequently crossed with the local unimproved type (which was, according to Davis in 1794, probably white) around Axford in Wiltshire, near the Berkshire/Hampshire border. Lawrence considered that the smaller type of Berkshire around at the end of the eighteenth century, along with the Oxford (considered to be a corruption of Axford and, conveniently, found in the county of Oxfordshire), was descended from this cross. It may have been that the red colour alleged by some to have been associated with Bakewell's improved pig came from this source.

This is by no means the only possible source of the red colouration, however, and Lawrence himself considered that the sandy or rufous breeds of England may have been Italian in origin. Rowlandson certainly intimated that the smaller and more

The European Wild Boar as shown by Youatt (1847). Many contemporary authors considered that some types had been modified by a degree of crossing with it, although Sydney in 1871 considered that this was impossible.

The Lancashire Hog had allegedly been produced from a cross with a wild boar, although this is improbable. From Holt (1794).

erect-eared Berkshires owed something to the Southern European breeds. Frost, in the *Pig Breeder's Annual* of 1934/5, referred to a red Indian jungle pig imported by Sir Francis Lawley of Middleton Hall,

Tamworth, around 1800, but he also stated that a large-framed sandy or ginger-coloured breed with black spots existed in Warwickshire and Staffordshire before this.

It is interesting to note that many authors considered that the wild boar had played an important role in the improvement of the Berkshire. In 1809 Mavor described how a Mr Smith of Letcombe Bassett had used a half-wild boar to improve the native Berkshire, and said that it had 'answered his best expectations'. Pitt in 1809 and Dickson in 1815 both mentioned that a wild boar had been used to improve the Berkshire, and Monk in his agricultural report for Leicestershire in 1794 referred to a Richard Astley who had a fine pig which was broad, had little offal and a great propensity to fatten 'very much like the wild boar'. Incidentally, Astley's pigs were obviously renowned as they were recorded in Northampton in 1809 by Pitt and as early as 1798 and as far afield as Somerset by Billingsley. Finally, the use of a wild cross in Shropshire was mentioned by Plymley in 1803, although it was not stated whether the Berkshire had been used. The use of a wild boar from Jamaica is mentioned by Worgan in 1811; whether this would have been similar to the Barbadian is not known.

John Holt in 1794 even mentioned a wild boar crossed with a Chinese, which produced small pigs but with good yields of flesh. Wilson described an emancipated wild boar from American of rusty brown colour that was introduced at the beginning of the nineteenth century. When crossed with the Chinese, a variety of coloured offspring was produced, some striped longitudinally with brown and black and blue, or black and white. Low's 1842 description of the wild boar suggests a rufous hue, and, incidentally, an appearance remarkably similar to his Old English. Contrast this with the wild boar of Youatt, which although described as dusky brown or iron grey, is not a bit like Low's. Low also mentioned that the use of the wild boar to improve marbling of the meat was being revived, although he considered this inadvisable.

Leaving the red influence aside, it is generally assumed that it was the Chinese and Neapolitan that had most influence on the improvement of the Berkshire, although Rowlandson, whose comments on Southern European breeds have already been mentioned, considered that only the larger improved types had been crossed with these two. Again the timing of this is disputed. Layley and Malden considered the Berkshire of the 1780s to be completely free of any foreign cross. However, in 1790 Marshall stated that the

These two pigs, owned by Chas. Butler and described as Berkshires by Mavor (1809), suggest that there was little conformity in breeds, and that names alone are of little practical use in identifying specific types.

Chinese half-breed pigs were in evidence, and therefore it would seem unlikely that the Chinese had not already influenced the indigenous Old English. It is surprising to note, however, that despite the alleged improvement of the Berkshire (whether with a black or white Chinese, a Neapolitan, or a red pig from whatever source) during the last few years of the eighteenth and the early part of the nineteenth century, there are still contemporary descriptions which refer to its long pendulous ears (e.g. Culley in 1807 and Lawrence in both 1790 and 1805), which suggest little foreign influence. However, Mavor commented in 1809 that the Berkshire needed to be crossed every sixth or seventh generation to preserve shape and quality. To this must be added the comment of Lawrence in 1805 that although the Hampshire hog was larger and fatter with pointed ears, it was difficult to distinguish it from the Berkshire (note his previous comments about the pendulous ears of the Berkshire). Saunders Spencer, admittedly writing over a hundred years later, considered that the Midland pig at the turn of the eighteenth century was long-snouted with prick ears – though this pig may not have been synonymous with the Berkshire.

It is possible that too much reliance is placed upon ear shape (as it is on colour) as an indicator of foreign influence. To cite Culley again, the pig referred to as the Berkshire was short-legged, fine-boned and easily fattened (suggesting foreign blood) with large drooping ears (suggesting more Old English).

It would seem that, despite uniformity in name, the Berkshire pig during the first part of the nineteenth century was anything but an established breed. It is obvious that the name Berkshire described a whole host of animals of different shapes, sizes and colours – which were in all likelihood undergoing continual changes. The two pigs described by Mavor as Berkshires, which actually came from that county, do not resemble each other much. Lawrence's comment in 1805 that 'everyone being spotted and having pendulous ears is called a Berkshire' is a useful guide to the naming of pig breeds at the time, but the perfect summary is that of Farey, writing in 1817:

the Derbyshire ... can boast of no ... characteristic breed, though some persons have distinguished the very excellent sort commonly found on the large farms by the name of Derbyshire pigs; others have called them Burtons and the Tamworth. I believe ... they would be called Berkshires in the Southern counties of England.

They were often white, sometimes spotted black and white, with erect or prick ears.

5

The Proliferation of Breeds

By the mid-nineteenth century pigs could be broadly classified into those of the large breed and those of the small breed. These, at least, were the two categories of pig judged at the Royal Show of 1858 at Chester, and such divisions went back earlier. Thus the *JRASE* of 1852 includes a table of all the previous prize-winning categories from which we can see that the separation into large and small breeds had been established from the Royal Show of 1843 (the first Royal Show was held in 1839). That size was of considerable importance in determining quality was evident from the attempts of many unscrupulous breeders to enter old and large animals in classes for small younger ones. Studies in the relationship between dentition and age in the pig thus assumed considerable importance, and show reports for many years to come invariably commented regretfully that many animals had to be disqualified due to misrepresentations concerning their age.

The large breed

Colour and place of origin were obviously of secondary importance, although the report of the show does make the occasional reference to them, and it seems that the large breed was predominantly white and based upon those types native to Yorkshire, Lincolnshire and Lancashire. Sydney in 1871 included the Cumberland and White Leicesters, although the former was, according to the Chester Show report, of the small breed.

A point worth mentioning is that size was very much a consequence of level of feeding (whether or not the animal had been subjected to a store period before fattening) and age as well as type. Thus Youatt mentions that the Yorkshire, improved by crossing with the Leicester, weighed anything from 224 lbs to 420 lbs from one to

A pig of the large breed from the 1850s. This was apparently a Large Black x Neapolitan and a possible forerunner of the Large Black of the twentieth century, although this example does not have lop-ears. From Layley & Malden (1935).

two years old, and could reach over 700 lbs if kept for over two years. The winning boar at Chester weighed 1148 lbs. It is interesting that the Old Yorkshire was seldom reckoned to pass 420 lbs even when fully grown. As the old pigs were of the Old English late-maturing breed, it could be concluded that the phenomenal weights achieved by improved pigs of the large breed were attributable in no small way to fat content – a point accepted by most contemporary writers and indicative of a foreign early-maturing influence on the large mature frame of the Old English. Such colossal sizes were not unusual.

Other examples of the large breed cited by Youatt were the Lincolnshire, Cheshire and Large Hampshire. Wilson included the Hampshire, Cheshire, Rudgewick (acknowledged by many to be the largest at around 1000 lb at two years old, although Middleton as early as 1798 recorded one of 1624 lbs) and the Northampton (particularly those from Naseby). Such pigs were used almost exclusively for bacon production, although it seems from contemporary records that they were all fairly rapidly declining in numbers as well as popularity. The Rudgewick was probably extinct by the time Youatt wrote.

Very large weights were recorded during the early part of the nineteenth century – a combination of age, level of feeding, the potentially large frame of the Old English and probably a degree of fattening ability from foreign types. This pig weighed 12 cwt at 4 years of age. Print dated 1809 (Farming Press Ltd; in the possession of R. Trow-Smith).

This particular pig, killed at the end of the eighteenth century at an age of $2\frac{1}{2}$ years, was, at 802 lbs liveweight, by no means the largest recorded. From Pitt (1796).

The small breed

The small breed was based almost entirely upon either the Chinese or the Neapolitan. In fact some considered that crosses between the two, as exhibited, for example, by Lord Harborough of Stapleford Park in Leicestershire, were the backbone of all small breeds. Examples of them at Chester included Fisher Hobbes' improved Essex Black, the Coleshill White and the Cumberland White. Youatt mentions the improved Suffolk (224 lbs at fifteen months) and Essex, and Wilson includes the Sussex, the Modern Essex, the Suffolk and 'the small white English hog ... particularly abundant in the Northern Counties'. All the small breeds were invariably described as improved and the result of a considerable degree of foreign influence. As such they fattened much sooner than examples of the large breed (and thus tended to be used for pork) but did not achieve the same weights, as they lacked the frame. In fact their great aptitude for fattening occasionally resulted in animals suffocating due to their excessive body weight.

It was generally accepted that all the black pigs around at this time owed most to the Neapolitan, with, possibly, some black Chinese (which was imported in the 1790s, as far apart as Lincoln and Northumberland). Trow-Smith considered that the Portuguese pig had been used, although Sydney was of the opinion that all the black pigs found in the Mediterranean were of similar stock, and descended from the dark Eastern swine. However, descriptions of the Old English in the eighteenth century as being partially black should not be completely ignored, and Sydney admitted that 'Hampshire has an ancient coarse and useful breed of black pigs'. The first of many recorded importations of Neapolitans was probably in the 1790s by Western of Felixhall in Essex, who purchased a sow and a boar (Long, however, considered that the Neapolitan, although procured by the now enobled Western, did not arrive until the 1830s). Western proceeded to inbreed until the Neapolitan was threatened with extinction, although it is possible that it may have been crossed on to others, as Trow-Smith considered that the sheeted Essex had Western's Neapolitan blood in it.

The improved Essex

According to Sydney, Western then turned his attention to the Old Essex. Wilson stated that this pig was also sheeted, although Youatt claimed that it was white at one end and black at the other and descended from the sheeted Essex. Together with this pig and the Sussex (another sheeted bread, according to Wilson) Western incorporated some improved Berkshire blood and gradually bred a pig that very closely resembled his original Neapolitan, although it was both black and white and therefore occasionally referred to as the Essex half-black.

Although it is possible, therefore, that the improved Essex pig contained no Neapolitan blood at all, Long alleged that despite Western's failure to perpetuate the Neapolitan he did in fact use it in his breeding of the Essex. Certainly the improved Norfolk described in the *JRASE* of 1844 was from a similar crossing: (Chinese ♂ × Berkshire ♀) × Neapolitan ♂ . Intriguingly, there are the comments of Young as early as 1807 concerning a Mr Wakefield of Burnham, Essex, who was breeding Western's pigs to be all black, as apparently the white parts of the skin 'are apt to crack when they are feeding at clover'. No further information was given.

Whatever its colour or origin, Western's Essex Half-Black was considered a particularly good pig, and Young, again in 1807, thought it 'the finest breed of hogs that I have seen in Essex and indeed equal if not superior to any elsewhere to be found', a comment echoed by Wilson years later in 1849. It is possible that, owing to the similarity in appearance between animals depicted in prints at the turn of the eighteenth century, the Berkshire and Essex were very closely related. Western's breed was being used as a cross in Buckinghamshire in 1813, and it was subsequently used throughout East Anglia and the West Country. Young continued by mentioning Mr Walden of Maldon, who in fact claimed to have originated the stock subsequently rendered more famous by Western. Even the later improvements made may not have been of Western's doing, since Sydney claimed that his pigs were in fact more ornamental than practical and that it was one of Western's tenants, Fisher Hobbes, who was responsible for breeding the improved Essex (referred to by Long as the Black Suffolk). The *Pig*

Western's pigs, described by Young in 1807, occasionally referred to as the Essex Half-Black, although there is little in these two prints to suggest much white coloration. The resemblance to Chas. Butler's Berkshire hog is interesting, as is the presence of pricked ears, suggesting a degree of foreign influence. From Young (1807).

Breeders' Annual of 1939/40, quoting documents from 1868, described the history of Fisher Hobbes' pigs. Apparently he had originally crossed some of Western's Neapolitan boars with the original black Essex, but the litters were often black and white and the females often ran to lard (blamed on faulty digestion). The Neapolitan boars

Possible major developments in the early history of the Berkshire pig

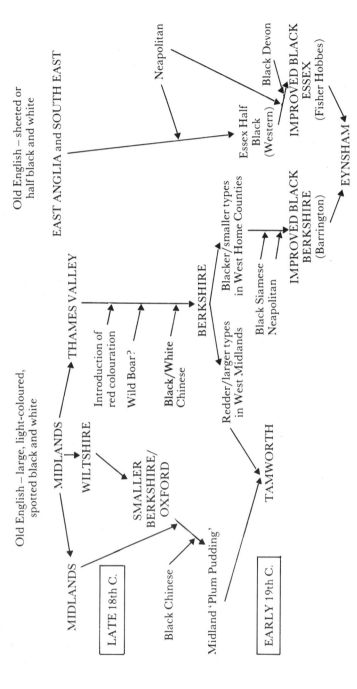

were then crossed onto some Essex × Berkshire sows, and the resultant pigs, with a small addition of Berkshire blood, became 'Fisher Hobbes' sort' (previously referred to as 'Essex and Oxford' or 'Improved Oxford'). The breed was achieving fame as early as 1840. By this time, according to the print in Youatt, Western's or Fisher Hobbes' improved Essex was completely black, although Wilson in 1849 still referred to Western's modern black-and-white Essex hog.

Further improvements to the improved Essex were effected in the 1850s, particularly by Crisp of Butley Abbey in Suffolk. Interestingly, the use of a new strain from Devon was considered a good introduction.

The improved Berkshire

I have already referred to the diversity of colour and appearance of those pigs generally named Berkshires – a situation which had not changed significantly by the mid-nineteenth century. The *JRASE* of 1854 reported that there was a great difference in types of Berkshire (although it was still considered superior to all as a store animal) and as late as 1871, Long was of the opinion that the Berkshire could be sub-divided into a middle and small breed.

Sydney, writing in the same year, described the Tamworth as red or red and black and, being hardy, prolific and slow maturing, related to the Old Berkshire. Modern Berkshire breeders, he pointed out, were most careful to exclude all red-marked animals from their breeding programmes – suggesting that the contemporary Berkshire could not yet be relied upon to breed true. Even as late as 1909 Spencer, in mentioning that white or rusty patches of hair were to be avoided, implied that such characteristics were not uncommonly found in the Berkshire.

It is interesting to note that the black colour associated with the Berkshire pig of the latter half of the nineteenth century (and indeed with the modern Berkshire) could be traced back to the 1820s, although the *JRASE* of 1889 considered that the contemporary Berkshire had been around since at least 1800. According to Sydney, however, Lord Barrington, who died in 1829, did a great deal towards improving the breed, and most of the herds of Sydney's time could be traced back to his herd. Barrington's methods were never handed down, but the predominantly black pig that he produced must have owed at least something to the Neapolitan, although Low

Youatt's Berkshire indicates that colour was not the only diverse point of the breed at that time. From Youatt (1847).

claimed that the largely black Siamese had been used. The connection between this improved Berkshire and the improved Essex was mentioned by many authors. We have already noted the obvious similarity between the Berkshire and Essex pigs of the early 1800s, and it is quite possible that their respective improvements followed each other closely. Indeed Long stated that Fisher Hobbes was reputed to have crossed the improved Berkshire on to his Essex pigs to impart size and constitution. Crosses between the two types were recorded, the resultant pig being called the Eynsham (according to the *JRASE* of 1854), which had an increased aptitude to fatten without a reduction in size.

However, from the pictorial evidence (see frontispiece) of Low and Youatt, substantiated by descriptions from Wilson, it would appear that the improved black Berkshire mentioned above was not a particularly common pig. Thus the Berkshire of the 1850s was generally considered to be reddish, rufous brown or tawny white, spotted with black or brown. It was intermediate between the small and large breed, according to the *JRASE* in 1854. It is possible that at this time this type of pig was called the Tamworth when it was found in Staffordshire. The Berkshire was by now regarded as probably the finest breed in the country, whether as a pure breed or as a cross on to others. Thus, for example, a Berkshire crossed with a Cumberland (one of the large white breeds discussed below)

By 1847 Western's pig was apparently almost entirely black, according to Youatt, although other authors still referred to the presence of white. As before, it bears a considerable resemblance to the contemporary Berkshire. From Youatt (1847).

produced the Solway, which gave both blue and blue and white offspring. These were excellent pigs, better in some cases than the best Berkshires. It was not a popular cross, however, due to lack of uniformity of colour.

The improved Yorkshire and the emergence of Large, Middle and Small Whites

I have already referred to those pigs of the large breed, usually predominantly white in colour and based particularly in Yorkshire, Lincolnshire and Cumberland. From the mid-nineteenth century we can trace the emergence of those that were later to become the Large, Middle and Small Whites (or Yorkshires). These three separate categories were represented as early as 1876 at the Royal Show at Birmingham, and by the Royal of 1881 the Large White was second in popularity only to the Berkshire. The Old Yorkshire, as the white pig of the north of the country has frequently been called, has been described as an animal of some considerable size, attributable, according Sydney, in no small way to the fact that 'nothing draws such a crowd of Yorkshire folk as a monster pig

Two pigs that were important in the development of the Large, Middle and Small White breeds during the latter half of the nineteenth century. *Above:* Samuel Wiley's Large White; *below:* Joseph Tuley's Large White. From Layley & Malden (1935).

show'. Heaton, writing in the *JRASE* of 1914, suggested that the successful development of the white pigs owed much to local shows and to breeders whose enthusiasm for improving pigs was matched only by their love of pigeons and greyhound dogs.

The pioneer breeder of Yorkshires in the middle of the nineteenth century, Joseph Tuley of Keighley, had by the 1850 produced a far more refined animal than 'the coarse mammoth formerly seen in our showyards and now found upon some northern farms', to cite the *JRASE* of 1881. Refinements to the Old Yorkshire by using the new improved Leicester are mentioned by Youatt, who also wrote of a Samuel Wiley of Bransby, who in fact kept only the pure improved Leicester. According to Long, Wiley (of Brandesby) had also obtained some stock from Mason and Colling from Durham (better known as Shorthorn breeders) in the 1820s. They were referred to as Chinese, and though they bore little resemblance to the original Chinese pig, there was considerable Far-Eastern influence. These pigs were claimed to be forerunners of the Small White, although Long also mentioned that there were a number of local variations. In 1849 Wilson stated that the small white hog was particularly abundant in the northern counties. The report of the judge at the Chester Royal of 1858 had also discussed how Wiley had apparently had a small white breed for fully fifty years and in about 1817 had purchased an excellent sow from Robert Colling to improve his breed. Wiley had retained a true pedigree of his herd from that date. Other notable breeders of the time were Wainman and his bailiff Fisher from Yorkshire, Duckering from Lincolnshire, and Lord Ellismere.

Tuley was alleged to have used Bakewell's improved Leicester in his breeding programme, despite many assertions that the Large White pig could be traced back virtually unchanged to the original Old English. Davidson, confirming the comments of Strickland in 1812, claimed that improvement to the Old Yorkshire started with crosses with the New Leicester (said to be a White Chinese × Yorkshire, and according to Davidson not to be confused, therefore, with Bakewell's apparently black Leicester). However, as early as 1805 Lawrence maintained that the Yorkshire, one of the worst of the old large types, was now being improved by the Berkshire. In 1794, James and Malcolm had commented,

It was with satisfaction that we learnt that Mr Benwell's [one of the London brewers] predecessor, Mr Bell, had some years ago sent a great many boars and sows from Berkshire into Yorkshire, which had succeeded so well as greatly to have improved the breed.

Confusingly, Long quotes an anonymous breeder who maintained that the improved Berkshire had originated from a cross between the original Large White and the imported black Chinese. Observations that crosses between a pure-bred white pig and the contemporary black Berkshire almost invariably produced all-white progeny may lend support to this argument, and to the possibility of the lengthy ancestry of the Large White. Finally, Layley and Malden stated that Tuley used a number of breeds sparingly in his improvement of the Old Yorkshire.

Youatt certainly mentioned the use of both the Chinese and Neapolitan, the Berkshire and even Lord Western's Essex as possible crosses on to the Yorkshire, although Sydney admitted that breeders of Large White pigs were generally unwilling to allow that their improvements had been based on Chinese or other foreign crosses.

Thus, depending upon the degree of crossing, several different forms of the improved Yorkshire emerged; hence the gradual development of three distinct types. Long commented rather uncharitably (although his opinions were echoed by Sydney) that the Middle White breed arose only because Tuley exhibited some pigs in 1852 which were too small for the Large White class and too large for the Small White class; because they were such good specimens it was considered inappropriate to disqualify them, and so a new class was established. Long cites an example of a white pig that won prizes as a Small White and then, as it grew older and larger, won the Middle White class at the 1864 Royal and the Large White class at the 1865 Royal. Contrary to this is the surprising comment in the *JRASE* of 1876 that Middle Whites were allocated their own class in that year for the first time. The confusion over which class certain individuals should be entered for persisted at least until the Royal Show of 1884 at Shrewsbury; comments from the 1889 Royal at Windsor suggest that it was still hard to distinguish Middle Whites from either the Large or the Small; and at the Royal of 1905 there was some difficulty over deciding whether pigs were Large or Middle White. It seems that size was very much an indication of the degree of Chinese (probably White) influence, although, as we have seen, the age of the animal was also important. However, Sydney maintained that it was fairly common for all white breeds to have pale blue spots which often increased in number as the animal aged. These may be evidence of a black ancestry (attributable to the Berkshire or Essex crosses mentioned earlier) although they were perfectly acceptable to judges as long as they were covered in white

The Large (*above*) and Small (*below*) Yorkshire pigs certainly appear different, with the latter having characteristically greater foreign influence, as seen from the greater amount of fat cover, shorter body and pricked ears. From Long (1886).

hairs. However, the judges at the Manchester Royal Show of 1869 did not appreciate having to award a prize to an animal with a partially black skin that had been exhibited as a Small White. By 1909, Spencer wrote that blue spots on the skin and black hairs were officially regarded as objections in the Large White.

Before leaving the white pigs, it is worth mentioning that, with the success of the Large, Middle and Small Whites, they soon spread throughout the country, and, predictably, assumed the name of their new location or owner despite undergoing little if any change in appearance. Sydney stated:

> it may, therefore, be safely assumed that all the best white pigs of modern times have been bred from Yorkshires or Cumberland and White Leicesters or both, and many breeds such as Middlesex and Coleshill etc. may be dismissed as mere variations of the white Small Yorkshire.

The confusion that surrounded the naming of white pigs is well illustrated by these prints. *Above*: the Large Yorkshire; *opposite above*: the Middle Yorkshire; *opposite below*: the Small Yorkshire/Cumberland. Differences between them are apparently minimal. From Sydney (1871).

Other white pigs that could be included in the latter category were Bedfords and White Suffolks, and Sydney continues by quoting an illuminating example of the pigs belonging to Prince Albert. The breed name changed almost yearly:

1846 – Bedfords
1847 – Bedfords and Yorkshires
1848 – Suffolks
1849 – Suffolks
1850 – Yorkshires

1851 – Bedfords and Suffolks
1852 – Suffolks
1853 – Suffolks
1854 – Windsors

However, in Sydney's opinion there was no real evidence to suggest that any marked change had occurred in the appearance of the pigs over these years. It is possible that Prince Albert's pigs owed something to Wiley's and Sydney accepted that the best Suffolks were those that originated in Yorkshire and Cumberland, had emigrated to Suffolk, and from there been transplanted to Windsor. It is therefore likely that the Royal herd was being upgraded by the introduction of fresh blood.

It is quite possible, however, that the White Suffolk had a more distinct history than this suggests. Accepting that the old white breed of the country was fairly widely distributed, particularly in the Midlands and North, references to White Suffolks are fairly common. Youatt described the Old White Suffolk as an example of the former coarser types that were once common, but 'improvements' using the Chinese started at least as far back as the last few years of the eighteenth century. Thus Young, in 1794, described the Suffolk as a short white breed having great merit, but lacking in prolificacy; comments echoed by Lawrence in 1805, who mentioned that it was a delicate pig, and by Gooch in 1811, who suggested that it was gaining in popularity. Its fame spread fairly rapidly; Worgan in 1811 and Priest in 1813 both mentioned that it was a useful animal as a cross. In the 1840s Youatt was able to write:

> on the whole, there are few better breeds to be found in the Kingdom perhaps, than the improved Suffolk pigs ... equal in point of value to the best of the Essex.

This apparently white sow, which appeared in the County Report for Cornwall in 1811, indicates that the Suffolk was a popular breed as early as the 1790s and already showed a degree of Chinese influence.

This Suffolk, owned by William IV, was apparently closely related to the Duke of Bedford's Berkshire! From Youatt (1847).

Even as early as the 1840s excessive fat cover was a problem. This Suffolk, allegedly the winner of the Liverpool Royal of 1840, probably explains why the White Suffolk soon ceased to exist. By 1886 Long was able to assert that no white pig was associated with the county. From Youatt (1847).

Youatt continues by mentioning that most of Prince Albert's Windsors were improved Suffolks. They were mostly white and were Suffolks crossed with Berkshires and Chinese – the latter cross producing pigs that were less coarse and leggy. Wilson cautiously noted that it was by no means an economical feeder, but its value as a cross with, for example, the Berkshire (to produce a smaller, lighter and finer-fleshed animal) was reported by the *JRASE* of 1852. It is highly probable that by this time the White Suffolk and the Small White (Yorkshire) were synonymous such that the name Suffolk was now becoming associated with the small black East Anglian breeds (i.e. the Essex) that were being developed, as mentioned in the *JRASE* of 1881. Long went even further:

> the only legitimate breed known in connection with the county is the one we have referred to and which is now distinctly known as the Small Black breed. The fact that one or two Suffolk breeders at the outside have, at one time, kept a herd of exceptionally good Small White pigs, which they have chosen to call Suffolks, is of no avail, inasmuch as they were identical with the Small White pigs of England hitherto generally known as the Small Yorks.

Long thought that the Americans' use of the name Suffolk to describe one of their white breeds was thus an error.

Finally, the Coleshill pig referred to earlier was white, closely allied, inevitably, to the Yorkshire/Cumberland (although Rowlandson thought that it must be descended from a Chinese × Improved Yorkshire), and bred by the Earl of Radnor from stock originally purchased from these two counties. On being exported to England it became, variously, the Suffolk, Yorkshire or Middlesex, depending upon the fancy of the new breeder. The name Coleshill may have referred specifically to those pigs belonging to the Earl of Radnor, but it is possible that the stock to which it referred could be traced back some distance. Like the Small White breed of Wiley, the Coleshill could be traced back to the early years of the nineteenth century to stock owned by the father of a Mr E.W. Moore.

'Manufactured' or 'fancy' breeds

Other categories of pig that achieved fame during the mid-nineteenth century were the 'manufactured' or 'fancy' breeds – bred and named after a person or place. While this description could be applied to a greater or lesser extent to virtually all types at that time, some are worthy of mention, particularly the improved Dorset. This was bred by Frederick and John Coates from Sturminster Newton (father and son), and achieved considerable national fame, particularly at Smithfield. It is not clear whether they bred the type jointly, or if two distinct strains were finally developed, as John Coates was quoted by Long as saying:

> my father has exhibited pigs in London every year since 1850 and has never failed to obtain a prize ... At the last Smithfield Club Show, he was second for the Champion Cup, which was won by myself.

An indication of the genealogy of the improved Dorset was provided by John Coates himself, who states that his father had been given a Turkish sow 'very hairy and of a wild type', which was immediately crossed with a Chinese boar (colour not stated); the female offspring were then crossed with a Neapolitan boar, which continued for several generations and resulted in the Black Dorset.

John Coates also mentioned that occasional crossing with a good sow of the Dorset Black breed (not the same as the Black Dorset), which was the former breed of Dorset improved by the Berkshire, was important to maintain the breed. Coates did not provide any further information, or any at all about his own strain – a reluctance to give much away is quite understandable in what was becoming a lucrative business. The *JRASE* of 1878, in its 'General Review of English Agriculture', claimed that in addition to Chinese and Neapolitan blood, John Coates used a black Turkish sow and also a similar type bred by John Smith of Blandford Peverell in his breeding of the Black Dorset. The *JRASE* of 1889 agreed largely with Coates' details, and included a description of the development of what it called the improved Dorset. It considered, however, that Fisher Hobbes' improved Essex had been employed, an observation that does not necessarily conflict with the possible use of the Berkshire mentioned above. These two, as has been previously suggested, were very similar pigs at this time.

It is interesting that John Coates accepted that crossing with other breeds was necessary to protect the improved Dorset from the worst effects of inbreeding, upon which the production of 'manufactured'

Above: Essex pig, from Sydney (1871); *below*: Essex pig, from Long (1886); *opposite*: Black Dorset pig, from Long (1886); presumably before an obsession with fat cover led to their extinction.

breeds of uniform conformation invariably depended. This was by no means an isolated or recent observation. As early as 1790 Marshall had described Bakewell's pigs, which had been produced by inbreeding, as 'rickety' or 'fools'. In 1809 Mavor considered that the Berkshire of his time needed to be crossed every sixth or seventh generation to preserve shape and quality, and Western's original

Neapolitan was allegedly threatened with extinction through excessive inbreeding. The *JRASE* of 1860 mentioned that a cross between the pure Berkshire and Suffolk or Sussex (to produce the improved Berkshire – all the names here are almost meaningless) produced an initially successful pig, but one that was hard to maintain and which deteriorated. James Howard, writing in the *JRASE* of 1881, claimed that Fisher Hobbes had resorted to a considerable degree of inbreeding such that 'in 25 years he had never gone away from his herd (and bred) from animals very closely related'. This was initially a very successful method, but many problems gradually emerged, including small litters of deformed pigs. Howard considered that the pig was more susceptible to inbreeding than other farm stock, and that to ensure fecundity, freedom from disease and strength of constitution, frequent changes of blood were essential.

Although degeneration was not confined to the manufactured breeds (in fact it was fairly widespread – there were frequent complaints from purchasers of show animals that their new stock often failed to breed), it was with them that the problem was probably most acute. The success of the improved Dorset was followed by a rapid decline in its fortunes such that it did not appear at the Royal of 1889 (it may by then have been absorbed into the small East Anglian black breeds), although the reasons for this may have been due to the Royal Agricultural Society's policy of discrimination against the excessive fat of these manufactured breeds (discussed in Chapter 6).

6

Wrong Priorities and Lost Opportunities

Obesity and other faults

The gradual 'improvements' in pig breeding that had taken place in the earlier part of the nineteenth century gathered momentum during the 1860s, when the demand, at least in the showground, was for smaller, earlier-maturing pigs with more fat. The first two criteria were consistent with a changing consumer preference for smaller-sized cuts (attributed to a more affluent population). But breeders' obsession with fat production (the result, supposedly, of

The Poland China from the USA is an excellent example of the type of animal required for the production of lard that was allegedly to have an important influence upon British pig breeders. From Long (1886).

American demand for pigs which could convert vast crops of maize into lard) took precedence, with devastating consequences for the pig industry. The over-use of foreign breeds had been commented on by Low in 1842:

> While we should improve the larger breeds that are left us, by every means in our power, we ought to take care that we do not

sacrifice them altogether. We should remember that an ample supply of pork is of immense importance to the support of the inhabitants of this country. England may one day have cause to regret that this over-refinement has been practised and future improvers vainly exert themselves to recover those fine old races which the present breeders seem aiming to efface.

That fat pigs were required for the home market was considered entirely fallacious as early as 1849, when Wilson described the ideal pig for the London pork market as weighing between 40 and 70 lbs (and usually 'dairy fed') with no more than $1\frac{1}{4}$ ins of fat. Although there was a smaller demand for larger pigs (apparently the demand in London was specifically for rather small animals), particularly for cured pork, Wilson indicated that most pigs fatter and larger than the ideal were processed into sausages. It is only fair to mention, however, that there were local markets for much larger and fatter pigs – for example the demand for fat pigs of about 350 lbs around Birmingham (which persisted into this century) was from those heavily involved in manual labour or (apparently) those whose work demanded the consumption of cold meals!

Youatt had also commented upon overfatness:

A premium would be far better bestowed upon the most useful and profitable animal – the one most likely to make good bacon or pork, than on those huge masses of obesity whose superabundance of fat is fit for little else but the melting pot.

Bacon curing was traditionally carried out in the winter months, and thus carcasses with large coverings of fat to take up sufficient salt were required, so that hams could be preserved into the summer. During a trip to America, George Harris of Calne in Wiltshire discovered a curing process that could be undertaken throughout the summer using an ice-cooled house, and a patent was taken out by his brother Thomas in 1864, entitled 'An improved method of constructing rooms or places for curing and preserving meat or other perishable articles'. More important, perhaps, was the perfection of a mild cure which did not require a large fat covering to replace the old hard-salted cure.

Pork and bacon production thus did not require fat pigs, but the obsession with fat still dominated as far as the breeders were concerned. That this was to the detriment of the pig industry as a whole is apparent from the many comments concerning fat at the time. Instructions to the judges of pigs at the Royal Show contained the advice that they were

> not to take into consideration the present value to the butcher of animals exhibited but to decide according to their relative merits for the purpose of breeding.

It is quite possible therefore, that the breeding animal and the meat animal were regarded as two separate entities. However, the judge at the Manchester Royal Show of 1869 admitted that most animals were in a state of great obesity. The report of the 1871 Royal Show held at Wolverhampton included this criticism:

> Throughout the pig classes however, there were many examples of overfeeding sufficient to render the animals unfit for breeding purposes. This is a growing evil for which it is difficult to suggest a cure.

This, amazingly, was preceded by the observation that the collection of show pigs was of the finest quality – it is interesting to note that overfeeding was regarded as the cause of fatness (which it was, indirectly), whereas no one considered the detrimental effects of continued breeding for earlier maturity. Further pessimistic comments followed from judges. This, for example, from the report of the 1874 Royal Show at Bedford:

> It is worthy of remark that a hot sun acting on animals whose vital organs were debilitated by an excess of fat produced the same effects as a thick fog on many of the animals shown in a similar condition at the Smithfield Show of 1873. It is to be hoped that this experience will not be lost on exhibitors and will tend to produce a less morbid condition of obesity in the animals exhibited at these shows.

The judges' report on the Royal Show of 1877 held at Kilburn lamented that a considerable amount of money was wasted in the production of over-fat pigs, as the population would not now buy fat bacon. There was a considerable diversity of opinion over what constituted a 'good pig' and a 'good carcass'. The breeders obviously thought only of the former, whereas the bacon trade considered that pigs were bred with little or no attention to what was required by the curer or consumer. Further confusion may have been added by another factor – witness this incredible observation by Charles Spencer:

> as [pig] judging was an added responsibility of the sheep judges ... the middles [in classes for either large or small whites] were generally put first; their nice square backs used to appeal to a sheep connoisseur.

The highest quality bacon came from moderately-sized pigs with no more than 'two fingers' of fat. It was thought that, due to the rough and most unsatisfactory marketing arrangements, the only way to improve carcass conformation would be by increasing the price paid for better pigs.

The judge at the Carlisle Royal of 1880 remarked that the tendency towards monstrosity and obesity in exhibition pigs rendered these animals better for the manufacture of lard than of profitable bacon. Similar sentiments were echoed soon afterwards:

> it is painful to see prostrate masses of fat grunting and sweating under a weary life in the heat ... the time has come to put a check on the unlimited exhibition of animals that plainly cannot be in a fit state for breeding (Derby 1881).

> all blubber with little of the lean flesh which is wholesome for man (Reading 1882).

> Would it not be well to give prizes for sows with not less than six, eight or nine pigs ... let it be shown that the model sow has the indispensable property of being able to perpetuate her species (Shrewsbury 1884).

It seems that some judges were still indifferent to the situation, and based their assessments upon quite ridiculous and meaningless criteria – although the following comment may provide a guide as to where some of the problems lay:

> The pigs in the various [small white] classes are principally noticeable for their superior quality, their freedom from coarseness and the fact that the prizewinners all come from the home farms of three members of our aristocracy ... this is

sufficient proof of the excellence of the exhibits (Norwich 1886).

The trend away from fat pork, due to a large increase in demand for lean and a considerable fall in the value of lard, led to the definition of the model pig by the judge at the Newcastle Royal of 1887, as one that:

> in the shortest time, and at the least cost, produces the maximum amount of lean meat in the best parts, with the minimum of low-priced or discounted meat and valueless offal.

It was noted that show pigs rarely conformed to this, particularly in terms of good development of hindquarters. The *JRASE* of 1889 observed pessimistically that:

> with the sole exception of the ability to fatten, nearly all the points of excellence of the show breeds have been improved out. As producers of lard they are unsurpassed but from the bacon curers' point of view they are fast becoming impractical.

Even in 1904, there were complaints about pigs being exhibited with too much fat, which obscured defects and rendered the animals useless for breeding, and in 1909 Sanders Spencer commented:

> fashionable pigs are unfortunately often bred solely for their aptitude to fatten or some fancy points which have little or no commercial value.

In 1871 Sydney had quoted a letter from a French visitor complaining about the average English pig, which when boiled left nothing but grease and lacked the constitution to survive French conditions. Sydney countered this argument by asserting that there were good pigs to be found, 'much better than those in France even', but not in the show-rings, where all you see are 'snow-white bladders of lard'. Overseas buyers were advised to give the show-ring a wide berth. It is possible that by referring only to official show reports, a distorted view of the predominant pig types of the time appears. However, the opinion of the curers was critical, and it would seem that the show classes were fairly accurate indicators of the breeds of the time. Messrs Harris of Calne stated in a leaflet in 1887:

we think that feeders and breeders ... cannot fail to be struck
with the disadvantage under which they are suffering through
their present breed of pigs being so devoid of lean meat.

Furthermore, statistics relating to the import of bacon and hams
reveal an enormous increase from 6,180 cwt in 1840 to 4,917,631 cwt
in 1879. The increase in pork imports, though not as large, was still
significant (from 29,532 cwt to 414,209 cwt). This was at a time
when, for example, the number of home pigs fell by a million head
between 1872 and 1879. There could be no more damning
indictment of the quality of home-produced pig meat than this.

Early maturity and fatness were associated more with those pigs
that were descended from Far Eastern and Neapolitan stock.
However, the association between these pigs and poor carcass quality
had been appreciated for many years. As early as 1794 Thomas Davis
had written that the firmness of the Old Wiltshire pig was lost when
crossed with the Chinese or Black African (probably the Neapolitan
or a similar type). In 1805 Lawrence considered that excessive use of
the Chinese produced only blubber with no additional benefits.
Wilson and the French correspondent quoted by Sydney had both
complained of the greasy nature of the carcass. This defect was due,
apparently, to the considerably lower boiling point of the fat of the
oriental types. As a result of this, biscuits produced from lard from
these pigs rapidly went rancid. However, excessive fat cover was by
no means confined to the meat pig of oriental origins, and
Rowlandson considered that sows during gestation laid down too
much fat (although this could have been rectified by feed
restriction), which he thought reduced subsequent milk output.

As well as being far too small and fat for bacon, and fit only for
delicate pork for the gentleman's table (the Small White, being
almost entirely Chinese, was considered flavourless), the pure
Chinese also had a number of other defects which it imparted to
other types to a greater or lesser extent depending upon the degree of
crossing. Hardly surprisingly, it was not well suited to the harsh
British climate. Boys in 1793 remarked that it did not bear the cold
well, and that such pigs 'are very apt to hide in stable dung and get
the mange'. Low considered that the Siamese was not a particularly
hardy type, and the *JRASE* of 1844 commented that Chinese crosses
needed to be kept warm, dry and clean if they were to realise their
potential.

Finally, the reproductive efficiency of the Eastern pigs, particularly

The Berkshires described by Long in 1886 (*above*) and Sydney in 1871 (*below*) indicate that the largely black body with white extremities was now more common. It is also evident that fat cover was becoming excessive.

in terms of numbers of young born and mothering ability, was comparatively poor, a point to which Lawrence had drawn attention in 1805. In fact he considered that Bakewell's improved Leicesters were liable to these objections. It seems that even the show breeders were aware of the adverse characteristics of the pure Chinese. As we have noted, Sydney mentioned that breeders of Large White pigs were generally unwilling to admit that their improvements had been based on Chinese crossings. It is interesting that, as early as 1803, Plymley in his description of the agriculture of Shropshire had mentioned that the Chinese was on the decline.

Apart from these numerous faults of the contemporary pig of the late nineteenth century, breeders themselves were apparently responsible for one other failing. Such was their obsession with colour and form, in addition to fat, that the *JRASE* of 1882 described how a Berkshire pig was disqualified from the Royal Show of that year because the white tip to its tail had been artificially produced. Although the instigation of separate classes for white and black pigs had been suggested by Sydney in 1860, to avoid possible colour bias on the part of the judges, the judge of 1882 commented, on what was certainly not an isolated incident, that productivity should be a far more important criterion than colour, form or fatness.

Excessive fat covering finally led to the demise of most of the small breeds. By the end of the nineteenth century they were being refused admission by the Royal Agricultural Society. Thus the Small Whites, referred to as 'animated tubs of lard' and frequently unable to stand for the judges, disappeared. In 1909 Spencer described the by then extinct Black Dorsets as roly-poly pigs:

> to prevent accidents from suffocation the pigs were supplied with pillows made from round pieces of wood. These were placed by the pigmen under the snouts of the reclining beauties; whilst the effort to walk out of the pens to be examined by the judges was frequently so great that the attempt was often abandoned.

Even as early as the 1830s, the pigs bred and exhibited by Lord Harborough of Stapleford Park in Leicestershire (Neapolitan × Chinese and described as 'splendid young pigs' in the *JRASE* of 1858) frequently suffocated through overfeeding. Despite the glowing description they were not, apparently, particularly popular with his tenant farmers. The Essex and other small black breeds (which, had apparently come under the influence of the discredited Black Dorset) did not survive long into the twentieth century, since, according to Spencer in the *Standard Cyclopaedia*, they

> suffered so much from the well-meant attempts of admirers to cultivate appearance from the exhibitor's point of view, and

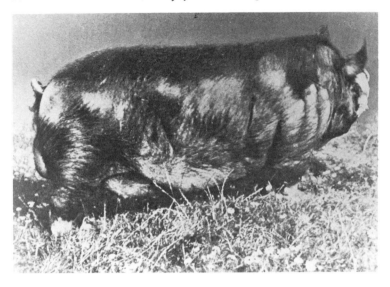

This photograph of a Berkshire from the *Rural Cyclopaedia* (1907) suggests a considerable amount of fat.

commercial value suffered to so great an extent that when the demand for lean pork set in strongly, the Small Black quickly lost caste.

Even the Berkshire, which in name at least had been the pride of British pig breeders for almost a century, was declining. A strong constitution, coupled with first-class quality hams, had been rapidly replaced by a pig with, according to the *JRASE* of 1881, a deteriorating lean-to-fat ratio as a consequence of crossing with types with a greater aptitude to fatten in an attempt to obtain earlier maturity. By the turn of the century, it was considered a poor pig and, but for the efforts of a few progressive breeders, would have followed the other small breeds into extinction.

The Tamworth and the Large White

The two breeds responsible for providing both the curer and the consumer with their desired carcass were the Large White and the Tamworth, although it should not be forgotten that it was, and had

The Tamworth. From Long (1886).

been, common to cross-breed to produce the meat animal. The origins and development of the Large White have already been discussed and, although some strains did not escape the attention of the fancy breeders of the late nineteenth century, there were those who appreciated the problem of carcass quality and began to pay attention to length, fullness of ham, leanness of flesh and lightness of bone, offal and forequarters as well as to early maturity. As early as 1881, the *JRASE* compared the Large White favourably with the Berkshire of the time (and went on to claim that the pure breed was a better animal than any cross arising from it and another breed – a fairly damning indictment of the remaining breeds of the time), and there are many contemporary descriptions of it as one of the most profitable breeds around.

By contrast, the Tamworth owed its popularity and success to its previous obscurity. Sydney had commented that the Tamworth was hardy, prolific and well shaped, but slow in maturing, and he added significantly that it was 'rapidly going out of favour with farmers from the want of aptitude to fatten'. The judge at the Birmingham Royal Show of 1876 described it as 'a curiosity ... whose snout was well nigh half of the length of some other pigs' bodies'. Tamworths were not a particularly widely distributed breed – the judge at the 1881 Royal Show mentioned that there were only a few remaining in the North Midlands. They were a very popular local breed, however, and the *JRASE* of 1866 mentions that the Old Tamworth was the main type of pig to be found in the Leicestershire dairy areas. They were even given a separate class at the Royal Show at Preston in 1885, where they were outnumbered only by the Berkshire. Long mentioned that a cross between the Tamworth and the Berkshire was considered most valuable and a practical breeder (as opposed, presumably, to one more concerned with winning show prizes), and he thought that this cross produced the most profitable bacon pigs in the country. There seems little doubt, as already discussed, that the Tamworth and the Berkshire of the early nineteenth century were of similar stock. The Tamworth was the name of the strain which was found principally in Staffordshire, while its more illustrious cousin caught and held the attention of the nineteenth-century breeders. Both Trow-Smith and Davidson mention the possibility that the Tamworth had originated in Ireland – Davidson suggested that it was imported by Peel in around 1812 to Tamworth. However, due to its relative unpopularity, it escaped the ravages of improvement of many other breeds (with the possible exception of a little Large Yorkshire blood which had removed many of its dark spots and tempered its russet colour to sandy). The *JRASE* of 1889 commented:

> By good fortune, the Tamworth was not crossed with the Chinese and now that the breeds which were produced by the admixture of Chinese blood have been condemned by the bacon-curer as carrying an excess of fat, this old, lean-fleshed breed will, I think, be as useful a cross in a contrary direction as the Chinese pig was some half century ago.

Two years earlier a cautionary comment appeared in the *JRASE*, stating that although the Tamworth had been increasing in popularity due to its lean meat production, its diversity of colour and form ought to be removed. This had been largely achieved by 1909, when Spencer described the judging of Tamworths and warned of the presence of black hairs and black spots on the skin.

Of these two types – the Tamworth and Large White – that attracted the attention of the minority of enlightened breeders who were concerned more with carcass quality than the show-ring, it was the Large White that increased more rapidly in popularity. In addition to the reasons given above, and the fact that the Wiltshire curing process could now handle whole sides with the skin still attached (which apparently discriminated against non-white pigs, although it should be stated that there was a regional preference for pigs of different colours), its success was also attributable to the rapid rise in fortune of the Danish pig industry, which had been based to an appreciable extent upon the British Large Whites (or Yorkshires). As a digression, it is worth chronicling this development briefly, if only to contrast the foresightedness, enterprise and overall efficiency of Denmark with an attitude towards pig production in England that can only be described as stagnant.

The success of the Danish pig industry

Dairying had increased in importance in Denmark from the middle of the nineteenth century (ironically it was the demand for butter from Britain that had provided the stimulus), and this was parallelled by the increasingly important role played by pigs, kept to consume the large quantities of dairy wastes that were produced. These wastes, supplemented with barley, produced an excellent diet for pigs. Germany was the major export market for Danish pigs. In 1887, for example, 232,000 pigs (together with large quantities of ham and bacon) crossed the border. The type of animal required was short, weighing between 120 and 150 lbs, and with a considerable proportion of fat relative to lean. Apparently such an animal resulted from a cross between the native Landrace (similar to the Old English, and probably closely related) and either the English Middle White or Berkshire. However, outbreaks of swine fever in 1887 resulted in Germany banning further imports.

The normal type of pig produced in Denmark was obviously unsuitable for the English bacon market (an observation that had completely escaped the attention of the majority of English pig breeders) and it was apparent that, if new market outlets were to be found, there would have to be a change in breeding policy. Such a decision may have been the result of a visit to Messrs Harris of Calne by Danish officials which quickly convinced them of the sort of pig required.

Three major factors were important in the subsequent revolution in breeding policy in Denmark. First, it had been appreciated that a cross between the Danish Landrace and British Large White resulted in large litters of pigs that reached a slaughter weight of around 200 lbs at a comparatively early age and produced bacon of good quality. The Danish Landrace itself did not produce such a good bacon carcass, and the Danes' knowledge of the Large White's capacity in this respect was limited. One of the more renowned of the home breeders of Large Whites was Saunders Spencer who, according to Hobson in the *Pig Breeders' Annual* of 1934/5, founded his Holywell herd in 1863. One of the pioneers of the Danish industry, Peter Morkeberg, apparently purchased several Large Whites from this herd (Spencer himself said that Morkeberg had visited Holywell in 1888 and 1889 – on the latter occasion to purchase Large White boars and gilts) although Morkeberg, writing in the *Pig Breeders' Annual* of 1926, said that foundation stock for Large Whites (or Yorkshires, as he called them) was obtained from many of the more important breeders. Layley and Malden even considered that the type used by the Danes was, essentially, the Large White of Tuley.

Secondly, it had been observed that although the cross between the Danish Landrace and Large White produced an acceptable meat animal, the use of cross-breds as breeding stock was largely unsuccessful. This was due to a certain extent, according to Clausen in the *Pig Breeders' Gazette* of 1952, to the uncontrolled nature of breeding resulting in considerable variation in size of carcass and quality of bacon.

Thirdly, the Danes had for a long time recognised the virtues of their old breed. Although several imports had been used to 'improve' it (using Middle Whites, Berkshires and later Large Whites), many of the pigs around in the late nineteenth century still bore a resemblance to the old type. Morkeberg considered that this was due to the market situation in Denmark. Thus most farmers purchased weaners rather than keeping breeding stock of their own. Those who were concerned with breeding tended to prefer those coarser animals with long ears, as they were regarded as being more prolific than the finer prick-eared type. They also tended to be better growers, which appealed to the buyers of the weaners. Thus the preservation of the old type was a consequence of deliberate decisions made by breeders and growers alike, and not fortuitous, as implied by Layley and Malden. They considered that the Danes had retained such a breed by chance – their agriculture had been so primitive in the early nineteenth century that they had largely escaped the use of the Chinese on their native stock.

The Danish pig industry thus proceeded along a well-defined path, governed by two important factors. The need to keep the two races (i.e. the Landrace and the Large White) pure was thought very important. Large Whites were obtained from reputable stock in Britain, but the Landrace proved more of a problem because of its apparent diversity of form. Agricultural societies held competitions, as a result of which the best herds in the country were identified by committees. It was sometimes difficult to select Landrace pigs that were totally free of Large White blood, but Clausen claimed that no Large White animals had been used on the Landrace since 1895. The criteria for selection were both the reproductive efficiency and the appearance of the offspring. Although Morkeberg accepted that there were setbacks, frequently due to ignorance of pedigree, the Landrace was gradually upgraded. Breeding centres were established, financed partly by government grant, to produce females which were then crossed with Large White boars, similarly selected, to produce the bacon pig. Complementary to these developments was the selection and improvement of the Danish Landrace bacon type, which would ultimately remove the need to use the Large White as a cross. In 1898 there were 69 breeding centres for the Landrace, a figure which rapidly increased to 190 by 1929.

The second important factor in the success of the Danish pig industry was measurement of carcass quality (as opposed to visual assessment of the animal's worth), which was to become an integral part of the selection programme. Progeny testing, initiated in 1896, consisted of recording the performance and subsequent carcass quality of four litter-mates (being two gilts and two castrated males). As such tests were carried out on individual farms, comparisons were difficult, and this led to the establishment of testing stations (where nutritional and environmental conditions could be standardised) – the first was formed at Elseminde in 1907, financed partly by the state and partly by the Co-operative Bacon Factories (themselves financed by levy). By 1924 Denmark was exporting almost 4 million cwt of bacon annually to England – representing 99 per cent of her exports and 50 per cent of English imports of that product – an indication of the success of the Danish operation. To complete the picture, pig discussion groups, useful as a means of relaying new information and exchanging views and opinions, were becoming commonplace, in contrast to their virtual absence in England.

The English pig industry

In fact the situation in England could hardly have been more different. It would seem that the average pig producer stood idly by while overseas competitors were rapidly intensifying their industry. By 1897 the total quantity of imported pig meat was approximately 6.4 million cwt, and the *JRASE* of 1898 commented that it was astonishing that England, which consumed enormous quantities of bacon, should possess so few factories (Denmark had 60 slaughter-houses in 1909, which presumably also served as curing factories, 36 of which were worked on co-operative lines). In response to the increasing demand for lean bacon, a quality control measurement was introduced into England in 1893 which laid down the maximum permissible depth of fat in any part of the back as $2\frac{1}{4}$ ins.

In an article in the *JRASE* of 1907, John Harris, of the famous Wiltshire firm of bacon curers, described how this development had been accompanied by the circulation of a number of pedigree boars throughout the West Country (paid for by the firm) together with the distribution of leaflets to urge farmers to produce pigs that would provide good bacon (ideally a Large White boar crossed with a Berkshire sow – the choice of dam being strange in view of the reputation of the breed for early maturity). Harris considered that the results of these actions were extremely successful (he was able to comment that the overall quality of English bacon had now never been better) – so much so that the carcass quality measurement was abolished in 1907! The continuing need both to monitor and to improve carcass quality by selection had obviously not been appreciated. Great Britain had to wait until 1927 before anything remotely approaching the Danish pig-testing stations was established – at Edinburgh.

Admittedly, there were factors other than breed that put the home bacon industry at a relative disadvantage. The cheap and plentiful supply of dairy wastes in Denmark in contrast to expensive foodstuffs in England was obviously important. Harris also criticised the costs of transport: the state railway in Denmark could transport bacon 200 miles to the ports for 10*s* per ton, whereas the same price would be paid for an 18-mile trip in England. Bacon could be moved from

Chicago to London via the ports of New York and Liverpool more cheaply than Messrs Harris could transport it from the west of England to Edinburgh. British exports were also hampered by the cost of transport: shipping bacon from New York to Cape Town cost less than half as much as the trip from Southampton to Cape Town.

Harris continued by complimenting the state-financed experimental stations and agricultural colleges in, for example, Denmark, which were regarded as superior to the usual privately owned and run establishments in England. Overall, it was hardly surprising that bacon production in England was not competitive.

The position was not one of complete gloom and despondency – both Harris and Wilson, who wrote in the *JRASE* of the same year, attempted to convey an air of optimism. Marketing co-operatives were being established (a good example being the Eastern Counties Farmers' Co-operative Association, formed just after the turn of the century) to by-pass the lottery of the open market to match, both qualitatively and quantitatively, demand with supply more accurately. The high costs of foodstuffs and transport could be circumvented. The largest pig-holding county in 1907 (even though it had not one bacon factory and few dairy farms), was Suffolk, where local farmers were able to collect their grain supplies directly from the inland port of Ipswich. The plentiful supply of wheat straw was useful, not least because of the quantities of farmyard manure that could be returned to the arable enterprises.

However, the overall situation was not particularly healthy. From breeding policy to marketing and bacon quality, the British pig industry did not compare well with many overseas competitors. Moreover an intense, even petty, inter-breed rivalry, based on esthetic rather than practical grounds, was preoccupying breeders whose thoughts ought to have concentrated on more important things.

The position had not improved by the time that James Long wrote in the *Pig Breeders' Annual* of 1923. Beginning with the observation that England produced the best pigs in the world (export of high-class stock had laid the foundation for many an overseas pig industry), he considered it ironic that the country provided pure stock of first-class quality in order that other countries could export bacon and hams back. The total quantities of imported pig meat were approximately 50 per cent of overall consumption, and Long attributed this to an amazing apathy on the part of farmers in breeding high-class pigs. He emphasised the need to employ only pedigree stock and considered that there was no virtue in a particular colour. He advocated an extension of the Bacon Factory System which, due to the bonus paid for bacon-type pigs, would encourage the breeding of quality animals. Finally, in concluding that more pigs of the right type were required, Long conceded that progress would be limited if farmers ignored the facts.

7

Changes in Feeding and Management

Right from the start, the prime objective of the 'improvers', apart
from satisfying their curiosity, was to breed out the slow-growing,
late-maturing characteristics of the Old English and replace it with a
pig that would fatten much more rapidly: a more profitable feeder.
The development of new breed types, however, should be viewed
alongside the gradual changes in feeding and management that were
taking place throughout the nineteenth century. In fact breeding and
feeding can be regarded as complementary processes. It has been
argued that the changes in the lifestyle of the pig from open foraging
in woods or scavenging in towns to relative confinement allowed the
introduction of the less hardy breeds of the Mediterranean and Far
East. These in turn could only realise their potential for rapid fat
production and early maturity if there was some appreciation of
which feeds to use.

Confinement of pigs was thus directly responsible for an increased
awareness of the value of feeds. Pigs free to roam, at least during the
fattening stage, would have access to an enormous variety of food,
giving a balanced diet that would in all probability supply the
necessary elements for health and growth. Those animals not
allowed to forage were entirely dependent upon the farmer for their
food, and deficiency diseases, such as rickets, became increasingly
common as a result of ignorance of nutritional requirements. It
could be argued that knowledge of nutrition was (and probably still
is) a major limitation on intensive pig keeping. Moreover, pigs
allowed to roam, presumably with access to a wide range of
foodstuffs, were considered better and their meat sweeter than
sty-fed animals as early as 1726, according to the *Dictionarium
Rusticum* of that year. As late as 1923 Long advocated grazing, and it
was certainly becoming common practice at the turn of the century
to revert to a pastoral form of rearing, where pigs were folded like
sheep on kale or clover swards. Even today the outdoor management

of pigs has many advocates.

We should note that there was no nationwide replacement of extensive foraging by the rearing of pigs under more confined conditions. Whether or not pigs were allowed to forage depended more on the type of pig rather than on the availability of feeds. Youatt wrote that pig feeding was dependent upon many factors: the circumstances of the owner, which feeds were available, the season of the year and the purpose for which the animal was intended. Rowlandson considered that those early maturing pigs (i.e. those with a considerable amount of foreign influence) destined for sucking pigs should never be allowed to run free, while those for pork production should only be allowed sufficient exercise to maintain health. Pigs that were kept for bacon manufacture (i.e. the late maturing ones – bearing much more resemblance to the Old English) were frequently allowed access to clover and grass swards, or to arable land, where they were particularly valuable in gleaning after harvest. This 'store' period before fattening was considered essential in the development of a large enough frame to sustain the increase in body weight, although too much exercise during fattening itself was not recommended. The grazing activities of store pigs were also thought useful in controlling arable weeds.

The seasonality of pig production, referred to earlier, was also an important determinant of feeding policy. Fattening was only really possible during the autumn when there was an abundance of food, although the importance of pannage was declining. In the nineteenth century there was still a seasonal basis to pig keeping. Thus the *JRASE* of 1844, in one of many examples, mentioned that those born in the spring would be stored until they were twelve months old, and then fed on dairy wastes until the final finishing period of around six weeks, when barley or potatoes would be added to the diet, and then slaughtered at around 240 lbs during September at an age of about 21 months – any later, and problems of food shortage would arise. Pigs born in the autumn would be of little use and would be sold off young unless they were fattened specifically for sucking pigs. The production of large store animals, or of small sucking pigs would, of course, require animals of different background. Rowlandson advised against any farrowings during the period from October to February, unless sucking pigs were the aim.

The quantity of food eaten during fattening could be quite considerable. A Berkshire hog of 1852 was put up to fatten on 1 June.

By slaughter on 31 December at a weight of 32 score lbs, it had consumed:

40 bushels of barley
6 bushels of beans
8 bushels of peas
2 cwt of pollards
2 tons of boiled mangolds
$1\frac{1}{2}$ cwt of potatoes.

Cold weather after slaughter in the autumn allowed people more time and flexibility in disposing of the carcass. Before the advent of the mild cure and the use of refrigeration, it was extremely difficult to preserve meat for any length of time during warmer weather.

Due to the almost universal practice of having a store period before fattening, a thriving industry based upon the sale and purchase of these animals developed. The great London brewers and starch manufacturers purchased many of their stores from Berkshire, and Pembrokeshire supplied many store animals to English drovers. The *JRASE* of 1854 mentioned a localised trade in which pigs were bred in Berkshire, stored in Oxfordshire and fattened in Buckinghamshire. On a smaller scale, but nevertheless an equally important one, it should be remembered that pig-fattening still took place very much on a 'per cottage' basis. A pig was considered essential to every cottage household. In Cobbett's opinion,

A couple of flitches of bacon are worth fifty thousand Methodist sermons and religious tracts. The sight of them on the rack tends more to keep a man from poaching and stealing than whole volumes of penal statutes, though assisted by the hulks and the gibbet.

Until the middle of the nineteenth century, the feeding of pigs was rather haphazard. There was little appreciation of the relative nutritive value of the available feeds, although it was understood that certain types were better suited to specific functions than others. Thus, for example, for the rapidly fattened pork pig, milk by-products were generally accepted as being of good quality. Youatt considered that the 'excellence of dairy fed pork [is] incontestable'. For the larger animals that progressed through the common rearing, storing and fattening phases before slaughter there was a large variety of feeds available. White had written in 1828 that pigs 'possess digestive organs of great strength', and this probably explains why there were so many different feeding systems. As late as 1878 the *JRASE* remarked that 'the varieties of practices in feeding pigs are innumerable'.

Grazing was widespread during the late spring and summer, but was rarely used actually to fatten the animal. Permanent pastures specifically for pigs were established, consisting of a variety of grasses, clovers and vetches; lucerne was considered superior by many, although there was a risk of bloat with excessive or too rapid consumption. It was generally considered that the best fattening feeds were cereals (particularly barley), potatoes, and peas and beans, though there was frequent argument as to their relative merits. Thus the quality of meat from pea and bean fed animals was sometimes thought too firm – due, it was thought, to the high tannin content of these feeds (a criticism also of acorns). Potatoes, on the other hand, according to the *JRASE* of 1844, produced a fat with a tallowy appearance if they were the only feed used. Some advocated a mixture of these three main feeds (in equal proportions) which, with the benefit of hindsight, would have provided a more balanced diet. Processing of feeds was often recommended, particularly potatoes, which needed to be steamed before use.

It seems, however, that the major determinant of feeding policy was the cost and availability of the various feeds. The potato crop was unpredictable, largely because of blight, and although alternatives such as swedes and mangolds were frequently considered (despite the fact that many root crops suffered from low dry matter content and high levels of fibre), the profitability of pig production was closely linked to the cost of potatoes. The *JRASE* of 1849 remarked that pigs were 'great consumers, and now that potatoes are scarce, it is found unprofitable to feed them'. The feeding of grain alone was rarely practical due to relatively high cereal prices.

In discussing profitability, it is clear that the business of fattening pigs rarely yielded any financial benefits. This was not always the case, and where farmers had access to wash by-products (from the dairy or buttery, for example) then they could make a living. George Winter, in his communication to the Bath and West Agricultural Society in 1786, described a detailed balance sheet, reproduced here, in which the total cost of fattening fifteen hogs was equal to the revenue obtained from their sale. He added:

I have omitted making any charge for attending these hogs, as I deem the manure they have made equal in value to such expense.

Profitability of pig fattening
(Transactions of Bath & West Agricultural Society, 1786)

1. Store pigs

Cost	£	s	d	Revenue	£	s	d
15 pigs @ £1 (aged approx. 10 months	15	0	0	2220 lbs of pig (live-weight) after approx. 6 weeks fattening @ 6/6d a score	36	1	6
14 bushels barley @ 3s	2	2	0				
Grinding of barley	0	3	6				
1½ lb madder, salt	0	5	7½				
Flower of sulphur, saltpetre	0	1	1				
306 bushels potatoes	17	17	9½				
	36	1	6		36	1	6

2. Porkers

Cost	£	s	d	Revenue	£	s	d
5 porkers (March 17th 1785)	3	12	6	April 21st 2 pigs = 107 lbs			
Expenses at driving from market	0	1	3	April 28th 3 pigs = 206 lbs			
6 bushels of barley tailings, and grinding	0	16	6	313 lbs @ 6/4d a score	4	19	0
Coal	0	1	3				
44 bushels potatoes		7	6				
	4	19	0		4	19	0

William Mavor, in his description of the agriculture of Berkshire in 1809, agreeing with Parkinson's Rutland of 1808, commented that if farmers outside dairy areas could clear their expenses, then they would be satisfied with the dung produced. Both points – the value of dung produced together with the vital role of dairying in providing wastes for feed – were particularly relevant throughout the nineteenth century. Thus the first report of the pioneer nutritional studies carried out at Rothamsted and published by Lawes in the

JSRASE of 1853 commented:

> Viewing the feeding process as one of the chief means of
> obtaining manure, it is of the utmost importance that the
> farmer should be possessed of some of the principles by which to
> judge of the productive power of such manure, especially in
> relation to the composition and value of the food consumed ...
> In the excrements of the pig, we should hope for manure
> commensurate with the cost and richness of the food which has
> been its source.

It is apparent that many farmers kept pigs specifically for their
manure, as mentioned, for example, in the *JRASE* of 1854. The
position had changed little towards the end of the nineteenth
century. The *JRASE* of 1872 emphasised the importance of manure
production (see table), and despite falling cereal prices, Long
commented that it was still difficult to feed pigs to profit. The *JRASE*
of 1878 accepted that 'it is generally agreed that pig feeding does not
yield a profit except in the shape of the resulting manure'.

Profitability of pig fattening
(*JRASE* SS VIII, 1872)

Cost	£	s	d	Revenue	£	s	d
4 store pigs (150 lbs liveweight each at 10 months of age)	10	11	0	692 lbs pork @ 10s score (260 lbs liveweight each after 94 days fattening)	17	6	0
Attendance		10	0				
Slaughter		4	0	Manure	2	6	8
Food: 1327 lbs palm nut meal 668 lbs malt dust 116 lbs peas 1400 lbs turnips	6	13	8	Total revenue	19	12	8
Total cost	17	8	8	Profit	1	14	0

In 1919 Spencer described many orchard owners who fattened pigs
beneath the trees. They did so not particularly for the meat they
produced, but to manure the trees and also for the pigs to consume
the insect-ridden fruit that had fallen, and so control insect pests.

Despite this pessimistic outlook, gradual advances in the science of nutrition were being made. These could be divided roughly into two main areas – an understanding of the relative nutritive value of different feeds, and an appreciation of the animal's requirements. By the middle of the nineteenth century, Youatt was able to categorise the more important pig feeds in terms of their pork-producing potential. Thus a decalitre (15 pints) of peas produced 6 lbs of pork; of boiled carrots $2\frac{1}{2}$ lbs, of buckwheat 4 lbs, of boiled potatoes 3 lbs and of wheat 1 lb.

The French chemist Boussingault was one of the earliest to attempt to catalogue feeds on the basis of their chemical composition – he used the percentage of nitrogenous substances as a measure of quality. But Lawes, following a comprehensive series of experiments already referred to, considered this to be fallacious. The reason was, essentially, an understanding for the first time that the composition of liveweight gain in pigs was not constant throughout life. Thus growth early on was concerned primarily with increases in the size of the frame and musculature, but increase during the later phases was associated much more with laying down fat. Basically, frame and particularly muscle development were aided by those feeds high in nitrogenous compounds, whereas fat deposition was dependent much more on the non-nitrogenous constituents of feeds. Thus Lawes recommended a feeding system which would start by using mainly those feeds high in nitrogenous compounds (e.g. leguminous feeds such as peas and beans) early in life, and then gradually increase the proportion of those low in nitrogenous compounds (e.g. cereals and potatoes) as fattening progressed – an approach which Rowlandson had advocated, with no scientific support, some three years earlier. However, it is apparent that the relatively high price of cereals and irregular availability of potatoes, coupled with better quality manure obtained from feeds high in nitrogenous compounds, meant that legumes remained popular throughout the entire growth period.

Towards the end of the nineteenth century, Lawes' observations on the relative value of feeds together with an understanding of the animal's changing requirements had progressed to the point where Long was able to publish tables detailing the percentages of albuminoids (essentially protein – the nitrogenous constituent), carbohydrates and fat in a large number of available pig feeds. Further tables (prepared by Wolff) indicated the necessary albuminoid content of feeds during the pig's life.

Requirements for growth
(Long 1886)

Age	Liveweight	Total organic matter	Albuminoids		Amyloids and fat	
(months)	(lbs)	(lb/day)	(lb/day)	(% T.O.M.)	(lb/day)	(% T.O.M)
2 – 3	50	2.1	0.38	18	1.50	71
3 – 5	100	3.4	0.50	15	2.50	74
5 – 6	125	3.9	0.54	14	2.96	76
6 – 8	170	4.6	0.58	13	3.47	75
8 – 12	250	5.2	0.62	12	4.05	78

T.O.M. = total organic matter

It was becoming possible for the pig feeder to blend a mixture of feeds of known chemical content into a compound diet that would be of optimum quality for a specific stage of growth.

The fattening phase had long been recognised as being wasteful if allowed to continue for too long. In 1830 Rowlandson quoted an example of a sow that had been put up to fatten on 10 October. By the 24th there had been an increase in liveweight of 38 lb. Fortnightly weighings indicated a progressive reduction in rate of gain until, by the end of December, the animal's body weight had virtually stabilised. As the pig had grown, progressively more of its feed had to be used for maintenance. Thus time of slaughter was fairly critical if feed wastage was to be avoided. In 1886 Long commented that the nearer to finishing a pig was, the greater amount of food required per unit of liveweight gain.

As we have seen larger bacon-type pigs were invariably subjected to a store period before fattening, during which the animals' frames were developed. This process became subject to increasing criticism towards the end of the nineteenth century for the reasons outlined above. Thus those animals with larger frames would need to consume more food to maintain themselves than those with smaller ones, during any fattening phase. Indeed, the store period itself was particularly wasteful, as there would be little liveweight gain at all. Moreover, even the need to develop a large frame was fast disappearing as the demand for smaller carcasses increased. Rapid fattening (over a short time to avoid excessive fat content) coupled with a complete avoidance of any store period was therefore recommended as a more efficient procedure. This, plus the understanding that the composition of liveweight gain was predominantly lean in younger animals but fat in older ones, and knowledge about the relative quality of feeds, should have contributed to a far greater efficiency in pig feeding. However, as late as 1919, Spencer complained about the inefficiency of a store period, which suggests that it was still being used. It would seem that sound advice about feeding, as well as breeding, took a long time to reach the ears of those directly involved in managing pigs.

8

Recent Developments and the Role of Minority Breeds

In 1923 Long observed that although in his opinion the type of pig was far less important than its quality as a meat producer, the number of varieties had been increasing; the most important pure-bred breeds nationally were the Large and Middle Whites, the Berkshire and the Tamworth. The emergence of others does not suggest that they were newly bred. Like the Tamworth before, relative obscurity may have kept them from the public (or rather the fancy breeders') eye, for it is probable that their origins could be traced back many years. The establishment of the National Pig Breeders' Association in 1884 had encouraged the development, recording and ultimately the registration of individual breeds, which had therefore subsequently (officially) increased. The major influence behind this was the opinion of many overseas buyers of British stock, who frequently complained that animals they bought failed to breed true. The Americans were, apparently, particularly keen on obtaining only animals from pedigree recorded herds. Howard had written in the *JRASE* of 1881:

> If English breeders would, by a small additional outlay, commence with a good race, and pay the same attention to rearing and feeding as they do to other animals, they would well nigh double the amount of meat produced, and this at little more than the cost of bringing their present ill-bred animals to maturity.

It is interesting to note that the majority of the 'new' breeds tended to be of the larger bacon type, which had not been popular during the era of the fat pork animals.

The most important breed at the turn of the century was the Large White.
Above: from Spencer (1919); *below*: from *Rural Cyclopaedia* (1907).

The Middle White, although showing a tendency to run to fat, managed to survive the excesses of fancy breeders. *Above:* from Spencer (1919); *below:* from *Rural Cyclopaedia* (1907).

The Tamworth experienced a rapid rise in popularity at the turn of the century, but never quite managed to replace the Large White. From *Rural Cyclopaedia* (1907).

White pigs

Although most of the old white northern breeds had long since lost their identity and been improved and merged to produce the Large White, or Yorkshire, some had retained their autonomy. The Lincoln Curly Coat made its first appearance as a separate class at a Royal Show in 1907 at Lincoln (not surprisingly), and the breed society was formed in 1908. However, its history was long (whether as a distinct type or not is debatable: In 1871 Sydney maintained that the Lincolnshire and Yorkshire pigs were indistinguishable). Layley and Malden considered it possible that the Lincoln carried the influence of Bakewell's improved Leicester, and Trow-Smith claimed that the Yorkshire was a result of a cross between the Lincoln and White Chinese. In 1805 Lawrence mentioned that the White Lincoln had a curly and woolly coat – a description with which Wilson in 1849 agreed. Youatt described both an old and a new Lincoln – the latter had been improved to a point where it was considered superior to any but the Berkshire, with possibly a degree

Two breeds which emerged during the early twentieth century as distinct types. *Above:* the Lincoln Curly Coat (from *Rural Cyclopaedia*, 1907); *below:* the Gloucester Old Spot, which bears an interesting resemblance to the Old English (from Spencer 1919).

of white Chinese. Saunders Spencer in 1909 was of the opinion that the Lincoln had been around since the 1850s, and a Lincoln pig was commended at the Chester Royal Show of 1858. Spencer thought it a hardy and prolific breed and one which could grow to an immense size. Its meat quality was not the best, but it was ideal in furnishing land owners with satisfying pork and bacon. He considered that it could do with further improvement, and that the establishment of a herd book would regulate the considerable diversity of form.

Officially the Gloucester Old Spot pig has had a very short history as a separate breed. Its breed society was formed in 1914, but it had not been mentioned in Wright's *Standard Cyclopaedia of Modern Agriculture* of 1909. Its appearance, however, suggests an obvious connection and close relationship with the older breeds of the country. In 1805 Lawrence used the name Gloucester to describe the sandy pigs of that country – and Loudon in his encyclopaedia of 1831 called it an inferior (i.e. unimproved) breed, usually white with two wattles hanging from its throat. Youatt agreed, and added that it was once supposed to have been the prevailing breed of the country, before crossing with smaller breeds had become fashionable. It is unlikely that the modern Gloucester could legitimately claim direct descent from these types but its relationship with the emerging Large Whites of the mid-nineteenth century is more than likely. Thus it could quite conceivably be an offshoot of the main line of those northern types that were rapidly having all the black patches carefully bred out of them, which slipped quietly and largely unnoticed into the Vale of Berkeley.

Intriguingly, in 1919 Spencer mentioned an old-fashioned Cambridgeshire breed that was lop-eared, coarse-boned, blue and white and curly coated. The sows were prolific and good sucklers but, predictably, the offspring were slow to fatten. These pigs had been improved considerably by the introduction of both Large and Middle White blood, which produced a pig with an improved carcass, but retaining all the maternal qualities of the former. They were sold in large numbers to Derbyshire and Staffordshire and other dairying counties, and it is not impossible that they reached Gloucestershire.

Other examples of white pigs whose similarity to the Old English was apparent, but whose history was obscure, included the Cumberland (herd book in 1915) the Ulster (1907 – apparently suffering from too much attention to fancy points rather than bacon potential, and being admirably suited to a grazing existence since it had long ears), the Welsh (1918) and Long White Lop (1921 –

Breeds which were registered during the early twentieth century were often remarkably similar. These photographs of the Ulster (*above & below*) suggest a close relationship with the Cumberland (*opposite*). The photograph below comes from *Rural Cyclopaedia* (1907); the other two from Spencer (1919).

previously known as the Devon Lop or Cornish White). It is possible that all these pigs had some connection with the Landrace of Northern Europe. However the existence of breed societies may have obscured the fact that two separate breeds by name could have been

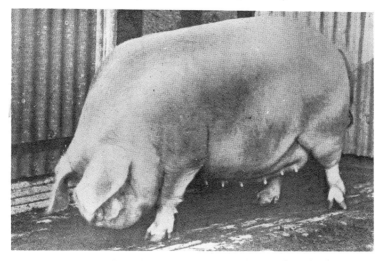

remarkably similar in appearance. Thus the Welsh pig had had a considerable amount of Large and, particularly, Small White blood. Saunders Spencer considered that the Cumberland had ceased to exist as a pure breed as early as 1909, and the herd books of the Welsh and Long White Lop were in fact amalgamated in 1926 for two years.

Black pigs

With the exception of the Berkshire, the small black pigs of the south and east of the country had been bred into extinction by the fancy breeders of the late nineteenth century. The Large Black, however, was very much in evidence at the turn of the century. The establishment of a herd book in 1898 was the result of the amalgamation of the two strains of larger black pig that were around at the time. The first was the smaller East Anglian (associated to some extent with the Old Essex), whose origins were in all likelihood very similar to those of the improved Essex Black (previously discussed) but which was not as refined a strain. The second was the coarser and larger black pig from the West Country – particularly Cornwall. Black pigs were preferred in the West Country, as their skin was less likely to blister during grazing. Layley and Malden considered them related to an old French lop-eared breed. By all accounts the two were quite dissimilar, although there may have been some tenuous links between them – a Devon had been used during the 1850s on to the improved Essex, and Sydney reckoned that Fisher Hobbes' improved Essex had been widely used in Devon. This, hardly surprisingly, led to a considerable amount of disagreement between breeders concerning the ideal form of the Large Black. It seems that the scale of points adopted for judging favoured the larger and coarser type – Spencer observed that Cornish miners were not so choice in their food as were the residents of London. Differences between individuals of the breed, according to whether they were of the eastern or western type, were particularly apparent at the Royal Show. The background of the judge was of considerable importance in determining which strain was awarded prizes.

Evidence suggests that the smaller East Anglian strain was kept in large numbers – the sows (considered hardy and prolific) being crossed with Large White boars to produce a bacon pig that was longer, better shaped, lighter on the forequarters and, above all, white. The diversity of origins of the Large Black was obvious for many years, and the occasional bronze glint betrayed the Neapolitan influence that had probably been associated with both branches of the breed.

The Large Black was probably a combination of types found in East Anglia, the West Country and possibly Sussex. From *Rural Cyclopaedia* (1907).

Finally, it must be mentioned that the county of Sussex was famous for its large black breed of pigs even into this century, but they were very similar to the larger examples of the Large Black.

Sheeted pigs

The two sheeted breeds, the Essex and Wessex Saddlebacks, both formed herd books in 1918, but, as with the Gloucester, there was no mention of them in Wright's *Cyclopaedia* of 1909. In fact Spencer, who was responsible for most of the pig entries in that work, made only a fleeting reference to Essex:

> The parti-coloured or sheeted pig, which was very general on the Cambridgeshire side of the county, was crossed by the Berkshire and later by the Large White; but the peculiar and distinctive colour still persists in showing itself especially on those farms where the owner makes it a rule to preserve [it].

They were by all accounts prolific and good sucklers, and when crossed with, for example, the Large White, produced pigs with both fine bacon and fine pork carcasses. Spencer continued by mentioning that the old Cambridgeshire sheeted had been almost wiped out by unsuccessful crossing with the Small Black during the 1860s in an attempt to improve its slow growth. Even in 1909 the Essex Saddleback (as the pig later became known) was restricted to the occasional sighting at a local market.

Sheeted breeds (as opposed to the numerous strains that were black and white patched) with a white saddle have been reported for many years. A sheeted breed was described in Huntingdon in 1811. Both an Essex and Sussex sheeted were described by Wilson in 1849, and Davidson claimed that the Essex, before Lord Western's improvements, was sheeted. In 1808 Parkinson mentioned a breed in Rutland owned by the Earl of Winchelsea that was black at both ends and with a sheet (and referred to as the Suffolk in London). The relationship between this pig and the Cambridgeshire sheeted must have been close. In 1794 Warne described a pig, unique to the Isle of Wight, as large, tall and with black spots and deep sides. Trow-Smith considered that these may have been forerunners of the Wessex/Hampshire. According to Layley and Malden, the pig referred to as the Wessex Saddleback was the only breed free from

Chinese influence (although it is possible that the Italian Siena may have been used). This was said to be because the relatively weak constitution of the Chinese and its progeny rendered them unfit to survive the rough conditions of the New Forest, and also because the locals did not appreciate the taste, flavour and consistency of Chinese pork. The Wessex Saddleback had originally been formed from an amalgamation of the Black New Forest and an old White Sheeted breed from the Isle of Purbeck in Dorset. Further crossing with 'another from the grain areas' (the Berkshire) produced a pig in which the sheet was confined to the shoulder. Apparently a group of these was shipped to the USA in 1825, followed by others, and they became the American Hampshire. Due to their high lean and low fat, they became relatively unpopular but were preserved by enthusiasts who managed to maintain them largely free of Chinese blood.

According to Layley and Malden, the First World War had had devastating effects upon pig breeds. War food orders apparently paid the same price for pork regardless of size and quality, and this resulted in indiscriminate slaughtering, particularly of the larger breeds. The Wessex suffered particularly from this, and at the end of the war there were very few left pure. In fact their survival was attributable largely to two families in the New Forest who had kept the breed for many generations. The breed was thus preserved despite one further important factor: the almost universally held opinion that white skin was better for meat production than black. Of all the authors who criticised the Chinese influence upon the Old English, Layley and Malden were perhaps the most vociferous. It is therefore somewhat ironic to read Malden's article in the *Pig Breeders' Annual* of 1934/5 on the Wessex pig, which included the comment that the trend towards length in bacon pigs was unproductive as it brought out the relics of the coarser breed.

Developments in breeding

Despite the First World War, many breeds of pig survived to be represented at shows (and others were, in all likelihood, around but not included). Thus the Royal of 1929 had classes for Large and Middle Whites, Tamworth, Berkshire, Wessex, Essex, Large Black, Gloucester, Cumberland and Long White Lop. The judge commented, however, that the diversity of breeds could be reduced with no real threat to the pig industry. Experimental work on growth analysis and carcass quality provided an excellent illustration of why this could be so. Although Lawes and Gilbert at Rothamsted had provided considerable information on this subject many years before, and the suitability of various breeds for certain specific carcass requirements had been appreciated for a long time, the work of John Hammond at Cambridge during the 1920s was definitive in its approach. He classified breeds into early and late maturing, their usefulness for either pork (which required smaller carcasses of around 100 lbs) or bacon production (which required larger ones of around 200 lbs) being determined by the point at which the rate of increase of muscle (i.e. lean) was optimum. In early maturing animals this was sooner at a smaller liveweight than with late maturing ones. Thus breeds could be classified into either early maturing pork types (Middle White and Berkshire) or late maturing bacon types (Large White, Welsh and Tamworth). The Essex, Wessex, Large Black, Long White Lop, and Gloucester were intermediary and regarded as dual-purpose. Hammond also stated that there was probably a considerable diversity in the attainment of maturity even between different strains of the same breed. Theoretically it would therefore be possible, by genetic selection, to produce the varying carcasses required for the meat trade from just one breed. However, the machinery for identifying superior genotypes was not widely available, at least in this country. In the *JRASE* of 1932 Hammond complained that the lack of demand for pork might be due to the perennial problem of excessive fat content. He suggested that the Danish system of progeny testing, in which the daily liveweight gain, efficiency of food conversion and the subsequent quality of the carcass of four litter-mates were used as a basis for selection, was superior to the British approach in which the subjective eye of a show judge was thought good enough. Not until 1952 was it considered that official pig recording and litter testing would be essential, and the National Pig Breeders' Association in its meetings of that year (somewhat ironically held on 1 April) discussed what arrangements would be necessary to institute a progeny testing scheme.

The Large White had been accepted as a breed of excellent quality since the early days of the century. Its popularity as the years passed increased, usually to the detriment of the other breeds. The table of registered boars shows the declining fortunes of many breeds, and the extinction of some.

The backbone of the British pig industry for many years has been the Large White (*above*), although the British Landrace (*below*) has achieved considerable prominence since the 1950s. Photos: The Pig Improvement Co. Ltd.

Number of boars registered
(Rare Breeds Survival Trust)

	1949	1955	1976	1979
Large Black	926	127	23	31
Berkshire	196	25	22	16
Tamworth	165	47	17	37
Middle White	157	52	3	10
British Lop	85	10	–	27
Lincoln Curly Coat	82	2	Extinct	–
Yorkshire Blue & White	35	7	Extinct	–
Gloucester Old Spot	34	27	14	51
Welsh	33	528	490	648
Ulster White	22	Extinct	–	–
Cumberland	7	1	Extinct	–
Dorset Gold Tip	5	1	Extinct	–

One breed, however, has seen a phenomenal increase in numbers. During the 1950s, when news of the success of the Danish pig industry finally filtered down to those actually involved in the rearing of pigs, there was a great deal of interest in the Danish Landrace breed. Unfortunately the name Landrace was regarded as synonymous with the specific Danish breed of what is in fact the native pig of Scandinavia and the Low Countries. Thus when Landrace pigs were offered for sale in the 1950s they changed hands for several hundred if not thousands of pounds each. The fact that they were Swedish Landrace was not considered important.

The current trend in commercial pig production, however, does not involve pure breeds but the development of hybrids. Boar licensing was introduced in this country in an attempt to regulate breeding and to impose a degree of conformity on to pure breeds. As such it was successful. However, pigs are ultimately kept as producers of meat, and the objective of breeding policy should be to produce an animal with the highest biological potential for such a purpose, rather than to concentrate on appearance and colour markings. If such an objective involves the combination of more than one breed, then cross-breeding should be a useful tool. With the abolition of boar licensing in 1972, the development of hybrid lines became a possibility and one that proved successful. It is interesting to note that in two hundred years, the pig industry has completed a full circle. Two hundred years ago pigs did not conform to any breed type, but were bred mainly for the local store or meat market. Thus demand dictated which sizes were offered for sale. Specific breeds

New 'breeds' of pigs are continually being produced. *Above:* the Polstead, arising out of a cross between the Large White and Large Black, was locally well regarded in Essex in the 1930s. From Layley & Malden (1935). With the abolition of boar licensing in 1972, breeders were free to develop hybrids which sought to combine the qualities of many breeds into one. *Below:* the Camborough is an example of a modern hybrid – bred for optimum and continuing improvement in biological performance rather than 'fancy' points. Photo: The Pig Improvement Co. Ltd.

were then established, merely by selecting specific individuals from a large population of animals, and selection became concerned with shape, size and colour to the point of obsession, encouraging petty inter-breed rivalries. Meat quality suffered accordingly. Today it is appreciated that points of excellence of pure breeds are of secondary relevance, and that the overall pig gene pool is most important. This provides specific characteristics from which the ideal meat pig to suit a specific outlet can be selected.

Commercial pig production and the role of minority breeds

The presence in the United Kingdom of a number of minority pig breeds, which have little or no impact on the modern pig industry, has prompted much discussion. As has already been mentioned, their declining fortunes have been regarded as evidence of their lack of commercial application. This fall in popularity is nothing new. The very early maturing breeds producing excessively fat carcasses rapidly became extinct at the turn of the nineteenth century. Even today it is those breeds that are early maturing (Berkshire, Middle White) and cannot be kept beyond a certain weight due to the production of large amounts of carcass fat, that are most at risk. The larger, later maturing breeds (Gloucester Old Spot, Tamworth), while still endangered, are relatively secure because they do not start to lay down fat until they are heavier. There is, therefore, a greater flexibility in slaughter times.

Unfortunately, in terms of biological performance (as measured by growth rate and efficiency of conversion of food into body weight) and carcass quality (as measured, for example, by length, fat cover and lean meat content) the gap between those minority breeds that still survive and modern commercial breeds is widening yearly. This is due to the continuing desire on the part of the industry to breed only from those individuals who show improvements in the characteristics outlined. This selection pressure is therefore far greater within the commercial industry. Comparative data on breed differences is almost non-existent, but a recent study at the Meat Research Institute in Bristol indicated a consistent superiority of the Large White over the Gloucester Old Spot in most aspects of pig production.

Above: the Orchard pig of 1821, representative of the type that was scattered throughout the Midlands. Although it is tempting to compare this pig with the Gloucester, direct lineage is doubtful. From *Buffon's Animated Nature* (1821). *Below:* what is interesting about the modern Gloucester is the way it has changed even during the last few decades. Currently it is 'fashionable' to breed for only one or two spots – a good example of how the whims and fancies of judges and breeders can influence appearance. Photo: Mike Potter.

	L.W.	Glos.
Final liveweight (kg)	96.4	96.9
Food efficiency (kg food/kg weight gain)	2.46	2.57
% lean in hind limb (mm)	78.7	77.6
Carcass length (mm)	823	800
Mid-back fat (mm)	17.8	27.9
Mid-shoulder fat (mm)	35.8	40.0

(Meat Research Institute, Bristol, 1979)

Furthermore, the Meat and Livestock Commission, in one of their performance testing programmes, illustrated the following trends (figures are the average for gilts and castrates although there were differences between the two sexes).

	Landrace	L.W.	Glos.	Welsh
Food efficiency (kg food/kg liveweight gain)	2.61	2.53	2.92	2.68
Daily liveweight gain (g)	765	755	741	704
Carcass length (mm)	809	793	758	806
Mid-back fat (mm)	16.2	16.5	27.0	17.2
Mid-shoulder fat (mm)	33.0	33.2	42.8	32.2

'

(Meat & Livestock Commission, 1981)

The report commented that figures for the Gloucester were from only one herd, and that insufficient groups for other minority breeds were tested to provide representative data.

The number of bloodlines within commercial breeds is far superior to minority breeds, and the rate of improvement is potentially greater the larger the genetic resources from which to operate. At the other extreme, some minority breeds may be so few in number that inbreeding within the small number of bloodlines remaining is unavoidable. Such a development is accompanied by a deterioration in the breed's performance (e.g. litter sizes start falling) and an inevitable decline into extinction. It might be concluded at this stage that there seems to be little that the minority breeds can offer in the context of modern intensively produced and marketed pigmeat.

Intensive and extensive production

It is when alternative systems of pig production are considered that the potential of some minority breeds may be realised. The capital costs of establishing an intensive pig unit are escalating and may be in excess of £2000 per sow. Interest in outdoor systems is increasing, and considerable advantages apart from much lower capital costs have been claimed for them, including better health status (other than gastro-intestinal worm problems) and improved manurial value of the land which could make the system a useful 'break crop' on an otherwise all arable farm. Climatic conditions are obviously an important determinant of output; extremes of cold and high rainfall are to be avoided. A freely drained soil is an obvious advantage. A number of problems have been identified, including lower output, less control over matings and higher feed costs, particularly in winter. Although direct comparisons are both rare and a little difficult to interpret, recent data from surveys conducted by the Meat and Livestock Commission indicate that, economically, outdoor systems have much to offer, particularly if fixed capital costs are taken into account.

Selective data comparing intensive (average) with outdoor systems
(Meat & Livestock Commission, 1983)

	Intensive	*Outdoor*
Average weaning age (d)	26	41
Litters/sow/year	2.23	1.96
Pigs born alive/litter	10.23	9.71
Piglet mortality (%)	11.6	11.8
Pigs reared/sow/year	20.2	16.7
Sow feed/sow/year (t)	1.145	1.209
Pigs sold/sow/year	18.9	17.5
Average sale weight (kg)	60.6	61.3
Average sale value/pig (£)	46.02	45.97
Feed costs (£/sow):		
Sow	176.63	189.14
Pig	408.07	372.57
Total	581.70	561.72
Other variable costs (£/sow)	51.97	35.51
Gross margin (£)	275.18	214.89
Gross margin/pig sold (£)	14.55	12.28

It is argued that the modern commercial sow is not suited to extensive outdoor conditions and that the breed required should be one that is hardy, independent, docile and of good mothering ability. It is important that the animal be able to graze pasture successfully. Lop-eared animals have always been regarded as good grazers, originally because they were considered capable of thriving on arable crops but also, today, because they are more amenable to control by electric fences. The British Saddleback is one that conforms admirably to these criteria. It proved difficult to identify stock of suitable quality from this breed until careful performance testing and selection programmes were carried out, based on current commercial parameters but keeping the outdoor qualities that were important. The improved Saddleback line thus developed is now an important component of the hybrid outdoor sow referred to as the Camborough Blue.

One further aspect of extensive pig production (which in this case need not be associated with outdoor systems) concerns feed input. At present concentrate diets are widely used in intensive fattening units. They are precisely formulated to meet the animals' requirements, and are capable of achieving levels of performance unthinkable even a few years ago. It is argued that both the cost of such a system and its reliance on feedstuffs for which the pig competes directly with man make alternatives seem attractive. The use of less concentrated diets may not promote high levels of performance but may nevertheless achieve an acceptable level of output. Such diets could be based on by-products of other processes (including, for example, those from dairies and breweries), which might otherwise be wasted. The pig's traditional omnivorous habits could again prove to be of considerable benefit.

Many have suggested that because the modern commercial pig has been selected against the background of concentrate diets, it is in fact not able to use these alternative feed resources as efficiently as some minority breeds, and the Tamworth together with the Gloucester Old Spot are generally regarded as being particularly able to thrive on low quality feed inputs.

Intensive systems themselves have been criticised on humanitarian grounds, and there is interest in developing alternative means of raising pigs which allow the animals to express their innate behavioural drives more fully. Studies at Edinburgh University are concerned with this problem, and while breed differences have not been fully investigated, it is possible that minority breeds may have a role to play.

Berkshires (*above*) and Middle Whites (*below*) are only present today as a result of the efforts of a few enthusiasts. British Saddlebacks (*opposite*) were formed as a result of the amalgamation of the Essex and Wessex Saddlebacks in 1967. Photos: Mike Potter.

Meat quality

Further characteristics of minority breeds that may be of interest include the quality of the meat they produce. Against a background of occasional criticism that the modern commercial pig produces a carcass that is somewhat bland, attention has focussed on the allegedly superior taste of meat produced from minority breeds. However, it is fair to say that post-slaughter treatment is an important contributor to the organoleptic qualities of meat. Those involved in the processing of meat from minority breeds are inclined to spend longer and indulge in more sophisticated curing techniques, and this tends to be reflected in the quality of the meat (and, usually, its price).

Variation in the taste of meat may also reflect the food consumed by the animal rather than breed differences *per se*. This point is particularly relevant in view of the fact that minority breeds are commonly raised on a wider variety of feeds, which may make a contribution to meat taste. The fact that they are on the whole slower growing may also be important. As with biological performance and carcass quality, there is clearly a dearth of comparative information, other than subjective claims, making it difficult to draw any conclusions. Certainly there are factors discriminating against the use of minority breeds, including lack of

The Welsh (*above*) and British Lop (*below*) are very similar – their respective herd books were in fact amalgamated for two years in 1924. Photos: Mike Potter.

uniformity, which may interfere with slaughterhouse throughput, and the observation that the dark-coloured breeds may leave a grey colour in the skin following dressing. The latter, however, may be of little importance as the risk of colour tainting of meat may be reduced if animals destined for slaughter are not kept outside, where they develop a much coarser scaly skin. In addition, meat animals traditionally have been and usually still are produced from cross-bred matings. Thus the use of a white-skinned breed in the terminal cross would reduce the incidence of coloured offspring considerably.

One of the major changes in the appearance of pigs this century has been a pronounced reduction in body size and fatness. For example the modern Tamworth (*above*) and Large Black (*below*) are much slimmer than their respective forerunners of the 1900s. Photos: Simon Tupper and Mike Potter.

Previous discussions have concentrated on the known characteristics of minority breeds and have attempted to suggest roles for them in the current pig industry. But future trends, for example those in consumer demand, are extremely difficult to forecast, and it is quite possible that some features of minority breeds that are as yet unrecognised or of little apparent value may prove useful.

The problem of future selection policy for minority breeds has been the subject of much debate. Although some Tamworth and Gloucester Old Spot breeders, among others, do select on the basis of performance testing or carcass quality to some extent, it could be argued that these criteria are not a useful basis for selection. This is not only because the gap between minority breeds and modern ones is widening but also specifically because the characteristics of minority breeds that are of little commercial relevance at present may be the ones with the most potential value. On the other hand, to have no selection policy whatsoever may not be the most suitable alternative, particularly if this is associated with breeding from stock that have genetic defects.

It is for these reasons that the collection and collation of comparative information about minority breeds is essential to their survival. The documentation of breed characteristics is very important as a useful basis for selection programmes.

Conclusion

It must be recognised that breed development is a fluid situation: even some of the minority breeds have changed markedly in living memory. At present, for example, the Middle White is being 'upgraded' by occasional crossing with the Large White (using those individuals in whom the 'dished face' so characteristic of the Middle White is evident). However, the loss to the pig gene pool of a breed which may shortly become extinct may be as serious as was the loss of its recent but different ancestor. Any move which seeks dramatically to alter the characteristics of a breed should be made cautiously, particularly as at the moment some selection programmes are following somewhat subjective lines, including an emphasis on 'appearance and beauty' – the very criteria that were responsible for the demise of the British pig industry at the end of the last century. Thus it is currently 'fashionable' to breed for only one spot in the Gloucester Old Spot, and the British Lop is apparently being bred for a more attractive ear! It would be most unfortunate if pigs were to be relegated once again to a position in which they were only of use to fancy breeders.

Postscript 2000
Current Perspectives

Some fifteen years have elapsed since the publication of the first edition of this book, and it is interesting to reflect on what has happened to the British pig in the meantime.

The commercial sector

There have been a number of important developments in pig production. In terms of size of herds, in 1962 over 50 per cent of breeding sows in the UK were in herds of twenty sows or less. By 1995 this had declined to 0.4 per cent. In contrast, there were no herds of more than twenty sows in 1962, whereas by 1995 95 per cent of herds were of a hundred sows or more. Although 'back door production', whereby pigs were frequently kept on a 'per household' basis has long since disappeared from the UK, these data indicate that concentration of pigs into fewer holdings is the norm. This economy of scale reflects what has happened in many commercial enterprises, and is not necessarily to be regarded as a retrograde step.

Welfare provision has been a key area of concern. Sow stalls have now been banned in the UK (although, crucially, not in any other EU country as yet – a recent item in the farming press described pig production in a well-known Scandinavian country that exports a considerable amount of pig meat to the UK – and yes, the sows were in tethered stalls!) and there are increased space allowances. Other areas which are attracting attention are raising weaning ages from the current four weeks (in contrast to developments in other countries where weaning at fourteen days is common) and providing ample straw bedding (again not really an issue elsewhere in the EU, and even less so in other countries who export pig meat to us). Outdoor pig production has continued to be a popular system. Interestingly, this has created a demand for well-qualified stock handlers.

What of the breeds currently used? Hybrid animals still dominate pig production, as is to be expected where continuing improvement in biological efficiency takes precedence over coat colour as a selection objective. Interestingly there have been imports of specific breeds from China, reflecting developments of over 200 years ago. The current interest is in prolificacy, and the Chinese Meishan is better than the current European white hybrids (ironically, the earlier imports were not well-regarded with respect to reproductive efficiency, but they were not from the same region as the Meishan). However, the growth rate and carcass quality of the Meishan are simply dreadful. Thus the goal is to introduce prolificacy without compromising performance – this is an excellent example of the benefits of hybridisation, *but* it also demonstrates the importance of keeping a pure breed (in this case the Meishan) with a recognised characteristic that could be of benefit in the future and emphasises the importance of maintaining a diverse gene pool.

Hybrids (i.e. animals that are not a recognised pure breed but are the result of cross-breeding to produce an animal which in principle concentrates the good qualities of all the antecedents with none of their deficiencies) are often referred to in a somewhat derogatory fashion. Leaving to one side the fact that the pig industry is currently dominated by such hybrids, it is pertinent to note that cross-breeding has been around for some time as the basis of pig meat production (see the 'Polstead' on p. 100). Debates on the relative merits of hybrids versus cross-breeds are of no value – they both have roles, as described above.

Although breeding programmes are currently based on selecting superior animals within a population (requiring measurements of, for example, growth rate; the assumption being that the characteristic is heritable – there is a good chance that a better animal will pass on this feature to its offspring), there is increasing interest in molecular biology as a tool in improving performance.

There has already been success with this approach, and an excellent example is with meat quality. For some time a condition known as Porcine Stress Syndrome (PSS) was associated with Pale Soft Exudative muscle (PSE) – this is both unsightly and results in greater loss of moisture from meat during storage. PSS was also associated with 'sudden death' in some animals. As there was an association between leanness and PSE in pigs, selection for the former increased the risk of the latter. However, the chromosome abnormality responsible for PSE has now been identified and animals can now be bred without this characteristic.

Molecular biology may also in the future allow identification of which genes are responsible for certain traits, thus making selection for these traits more efficient. In addition to performance, traits such as disease resistance are also receiving attention. Finally, molecular biology could also prove valuable in tracing source of pig meat. Thus claims that this pork chop/sausage comes from a certain minority breed could be substantiated with appropriate tests. The consumer is currently having to rely on the integrity of the supply chain. In all these new developments, however, there is still a recognition of the importance of maintaining a diverse gene pool containing animals who may possess as yet unidentified characteristics.

A further area concerns xenografting – the transplanting of tissue and organs for the pig into a human recipient. Against a background of a serious shortage in human donors coupled with the fact that the anatomy and physiology of the pig are very similar to those of humans, there is potential for this approach. However, there are fundamental issues relating to the health of the recipient and ethical concerns which need to be addressed. The value of the pig as a model for humans is also seen in studies of eating disorders – anorexic pigs are apparently not uncommon!

The pig has long been a key factor in the survival of *Homo sapiens* and the discussion above shows just how adaptable the animal is in fulfilling this role. There are those who might argue that the pig is merely being exploited by humans but, if the success of a species in evolutionary terms is measured in terms of its numbers and distribution, then the pig comes very close to us. Who is exploiting whom?

Minority breed numbers

The pig is particularly vulnerable to sudden changes in fashion, and breeds can rapidly move from a position of comparative popularity to one where extinction is a real danger; the more so when we consider blood lines within a named breed. Such a risk is more serious in times of economic crisis, as is now the case in the UK pig industry – minority breed keepers are not immune from the harsh reality of the need to remain solvent, and it should not be forgotten that minority breeds still only represent around 0.25 per cent of the national breeding herd. The 'fashion' for bacon from large breeds during the 1930s has been held to be responsible for the demise of many of the lighter pork breeds of the time, so this problem is not new.

Selection pressure was always going to make it increasingly difficult for minority breeds to compete with the modern hybrid on an equal footing, and it has to be said that sentimentality alone on the part of a few enthusiasts associated with an over-reliance on the show ground is not a sound basis for ensuring survival of endangered breeds. Thus the benefits of minority breeds need to be identified and quantified, to include outdoor hardiness, mothering ability and meat quality (considered below).

The Rare Breeds Survival Trust (RBST) has been concerned with supporting minority breeds and has conducted many surveys to monitor numbers. Such data are invaluable as a guide to the current status of minority breeds. The table on p. 99 illustrated the seriousness of the situation from 1949 until 1979 in terms of the decline and even extinction of minority pig breeds. More recent data allow further analysis of the problem (see the four graphs reproduced here), although the data are from surveys which are reliant on returns from breeders and therefore likely to be incomplete.

The Berkshire and Tamworth appear to be in a comparatively healthy state in terms of the number of boars registered, with the Gloucester Old Spot (GOS) recovering from an obviously parlous position. However, all three are on the 'danger list', with the Tamworth (along with the British Lop, Large Black and Middle White) being 'critical'. The other two (together with the British Saddleback) are

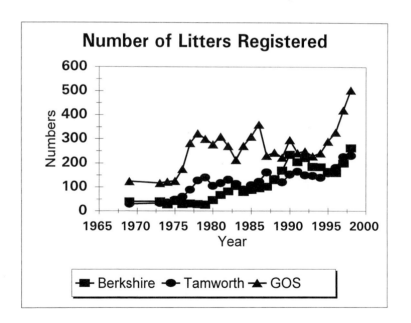

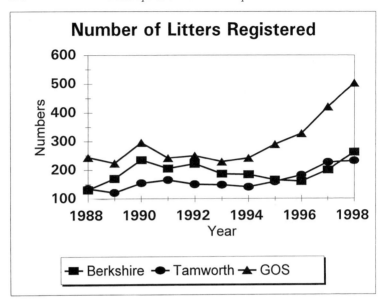

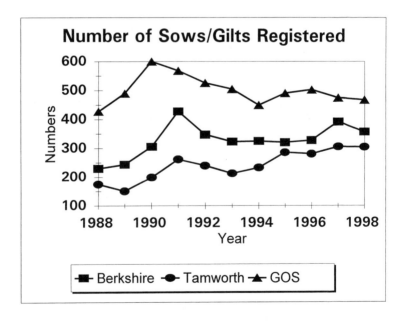

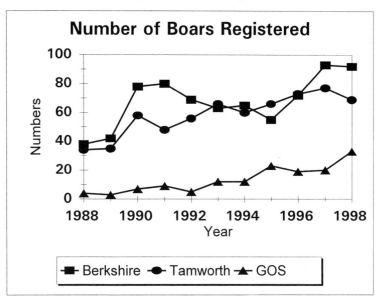

'endangered'. At least the figures are going in the right direction.

Further analyses are of the number of breeding females and litters registered, with the latter covering the same ten-year period and also the last thirty years. Bearing in mind the 'danger list' classification above, the overall picture warrants very cautious optimism – although the thirty-year picture shows just how close to extinction these three breeds have come, demonstrating the value of innovative developments from the RBST such as semen storage in the event of a major health disaster.

Meat quality and the future of pig production

It is in the area of meat quality that the minority breed has perhaps had greatest impact. National recommendations to the consumer on dietary issues have emphasised the need to reduce the amount of fat in the human diet and to ensure that proportion of saturated fat is no more than one third of total fat intake. The result of this is that the importance of lean tissue growth rate as a key selection criterion continues. However, there is increasing concern that the overall taste and texture of pig meat is declining and it is not impossible that this is associated with excessive leanness.

It has been recognised for some time, however, that fat in meat is important in terms of both the cooking and eating process, as it ensures succulence and, probably, tenderness. Although general fat content is important in this respect, the specific fat depot that is more important is referred to as 'intramuscular' – that which runs through the lean (also known as 'marbling' in beef). Minority breeds may have a role to play in this general area. While total fat content can be altered by how pigs are fed and at what age they are slaughtered, minority breeds are generally fatter than commercial hybrids. More specifically, 'marbling' fat is greater in some breeds, for example the Duroc from the USA (which may have the Tamworth as a distant relative). Identifying genes which control meat quality is a very topical area.

There is also a perception that animal fat is saturated. Pig fat, however, is half unsaturated and the fat within the lean tissue is in fact very close to the recommended fatty acid profile of fat intake by consumers except that it does not contain much of the very long-chain fatty acids that are important in the human diet (requirements for which can be met by eating fish once a week). Pig fat may be made even more unsaturated by feeding appropriate diets – the excellent 'jabugo' from Spain is from extensively farmed Iberic pigs in the Mediterranean oak forests (the 'dehesa') which are given access to acorns (high in unsaturated oil).

Meat quality is now also considered in terms of schemes assuring origin, breed and operating conditions. One of the major success stories with minority breeds has been the introduction of accredited butchers. Although it might be unfairly described as niche marketing (implying that there is only a very small take-up of an expensive product), this approach is increasingly important within food production in general. Volume production is being replaced by quality, and the minority breeds have been leading the way. Niche markets could develop further if the extremely large number of diverse products made with pig meat were to be more widely appreciated. It is pleasing to note the recent re-introduction into shops of speciality sausages alongside the insipid 'economy' ranges (which are, however, cheaper) including those from wild boar reared in the UK (is the wild boar a minority breed?), but this is only a start. The UK is a mature meat-eating market and no overall increase in meat consumption is likely. However, diversification of products on offer does offer potential.

The comment on the 'Iberic' pig above does perhaps provide an example of how pig production might move in the future with a combination of a specific breed with a certain husbandry system. The success of the extensive Spanish approach in employing the foraging activities of the pig (regarded as very destructive in the Middle Ages) might even be extended in the context of overall land conservation management – the omnivorous nature of the animal could be put once again to good use in the removal of weeds such as couch grass and bracken which are extremely difficult to control and shunned by grazing ruminants. For some reason, this appears to have been overlooked by a local group who, convinced that a flock of a minority sheep breed would look quaint on a hillside covered in bracken, duly introduced the said sheep – who now cannot be seen for bracken. A few Tamworths would have had no problems.

A cautionary note – pigs are still destructive to open land if they are not properly managed; the damage caused by recently-escaped wild boars to, among other crops, the hop fields of Kent is now considerable, and it is recommended that a wild boar is not confronted by unsuspecting ramblers. It is, after all, wild. If there are enthusiasts arguing for the re-establishment of the wild boar (and there is a proliferation of environmentalists whose chief preoccupation appears to be returning the landscape to nature, whatever that means), then a few well-positioned (and easily accessible) trees are essential.

Appearance

The changing appearance of minority breeds is evident and based on the current fashion among showground judges. Any glance through the photographic record provides ample evidence to support this observation, and it has been argued that such a change in itself is of potential danger in that it might be accompanied by the loss of a valuable genetic resource.

The previous chapter concluded (and, in fact, recommended) that it would be most unfortunate if the appearance and beauty of minority pig breeds continued to be important criteria for selection programmes. It is gratifying to note that, generally, there are progressive individuals who have moved on from this approach, but a word of caution is still necessary – the 'fancy' breeder is still with us and needs a rap on the knuckles.

There is one particular minority pig breed (which shall remain nameless – those in the know will recognise it instantly) whose devotees appear to be intent on colour and form, but little else. My comment in the first edition (see p. 111) that the British Lop is apparently being bred 'for a more attractive ear', which was intended to sound a cautionary note, has in fact been taken up enthusiastically by this other breed society. Thus suggestions as to future breeding policy are accompanied by comments such as 'too darkly marked for my taste' and 'although to my eye his ears are rather too large and floppy', followed by 'the first to go from the next generations must be any prick-eared pigs still lurking in the breed, closely followed by any that breed black and white or plain red piglets'. Apparently multi-coloured offspring are evidence of 'outside parentage'! Here we have a marvellous example of destructive tendencies of the 'fancy' breeder who cares little about gene preservation and more about prizes in the show ring and photographs in the colour supplements.

Conclusion

It is perhaps unwise to end on a depressing note, but it must be said that the UK pig industry is currently in a serious situation which is affecting both mainstream commercial interests and minority breeders alike.

The laudable introduction into the UK of improved welfare standards in recent years, resulting in conditions under which pigs are kept being perhaps the best in the world, has not been without its cost to the industry. The cost seems to have been borne almost entirely by the pig producer. Pig prices are some 30 per cent lower in 1999 than in 1997. I suspect that you are not now paying 30 per cent less for your bacon than then. Bankruptcy among pig producers is common and the size of the national herd is declining.

A strong currency has made imports cheaper. Ironically these imports are almost invariably from countries whose welfare conditions are inferior to those operating in the UK and where, accordingly, costs of production are lower, thus making the price differential even more disadvantageous to the home producer. A cynical but not entirely inaccurate view would be that large retailers are very vocal when it comes to dictating general production conditions (in the interests of satisfying 'consumer' choice) but are not prepared to pay for the increased costs incurred and seem quite happy to import (cheaper) pig meat produced under conditions that would be entirely unacceptable in the UK.

The label 'British Meat' in fact may not guarantee that the pig was indeed home produced – a whole pig carcass may be imported, but once it has been cut into portions in the UK it becomes 'British Meat'. We are frequently reminded of the power of the consumer so, when purchasing your next pork chop, do ask whether the pig from which the chop removed was born and reared on a UK farm. If the answer is no, then the choice is simple.

It would be nice to feel that a third edition of this book could be prepared in the knowledge that the British pig is still an integral part of the UK farming scene and that its products are as valuable to the consumer as in past centuries (and, indeed, millennia).

Bibliography

An important theme of this book is that the pig, because it is not the most popular of animals, has escaped the attention of artists and historians. Pictorial and written references are scattered everywhere, but they are generally confined to occasional sentences and paragraphs in texts concentrating on other subjects. Books written specifically on pigs are rare indeed. My major sources of information are listed below.

Journals/pamphlets

Journal of the Royal Agricultural Society of England, first published in 1839. Yearly comments, either on general topics relating to pigs, or specific comments on the Royal Show. The following articles give considerable detail:

1830 'On the breeding & management of pigs'. 1st S. XI p. 574. Thomas Rowlandson.

1853 'Agricultural chemistry – pig feeding'. 1st S. XIV p. 459. J.B. Lawes.

1878 'General view of English agriculture'. S.S. XIV.

1881 'Pigs: and experiences in their breeding and management'. S.S. XVII p. 205. James Howard.

1889 'History of pigs'. S.S. XXV p. 678. Included as an addendum to the judge's report.

1907 'The breeding and feeding of pigs'. Vol. 68, p. 64. W. Wilson.

1907 'Pigs & bacon'. Vol. 68, p. 71. John M. Harris.

1914 'The Large White Yorkshire pig'. Vol. 75, p. 40. S. Heaton.

1932 'Pigs for pork and pigs for bacon'. Vol. 93, p. 131. John Hammond.

Pig Breeders Gazette (1952). 'The development of the Danish Landrace pig'. Hjalmar Clausen.

Premier Colloque d'Ethnozoologie (1973). Institut International d'Ethnosciences, p. 523. 'L'elevage du porc a l'epoque medieval'. Raymond Laurans.

Bath Papers (1786). Article XLVI, p. 323. 'Experiments on the feeding of swine'. George Wintner.

F.M.C. News. Silver Jubilee Issue. Sept. 1979.

Pig Breeders' Annual. This was the official organ of the National Pig Breeders Association which ceased publication in 1939. A number of articles were consulted:
1923 'The position of the pig industry'. James Long.
1926 'Pig selection methods in Denmark'. Peter August Morkeberg.
1930/1 'Pig keeping ancient and modern'. Arthur Ruston and D. Witney.
1934/5 'The evolution of the British pig'. W.J. Malden.
1934/5 'The Large White breed'. Alec Hobson.
1934/5 'The Middle White breed'. John T. Eady.
1934/5 'The Berkshire breed'. Edgar Humfrey.
1934/5 'The Tamworth breed'. J.A. Frost.
1934/5 'The Wessex Saddleback breed'. W.J. Malden.
1935/6 'Reminiscences of Holywell'. Charles Spencer.
1936/7 'Pigs and pig-keeping past and present'. W.G. Coates.

Books

Agricultural Reports for England and Wales, drawn up for the Board of Agriculture. All the county reports contained the obligatory paragraph on pigs. The following presented slightly more detail:

Volume I:	Kent – John Boys, 1794.
Surrey – William James/Jacob Malcolm, 1794
Hampshire – Abraham and William Driver, 1794
Isle of Wight – Reverend Warner, 1794
Berkshire – William Pearce, 1794
Wiltshire – Thomas Davis, 1794
Somerset – John Billingsley, 1794

Volume II: Pembroke – Charles Hassall, 1794
             Suffolk – Arthur Young, 1794
             Essex – Charles Vancouver, 1795

Volume III: Leicester – John Monk, 1794

Volume IV: Lancashire – John Holt, 1794.

Individual Country Reports. Submitted as revised and updated versions of the Agricultural Reports. As before, all entries mentioned pigs, but these presented more detail:

Bedford – Thomas Batchelor, 1808
Berkshire – William Mavor, 1809
Buckinghamshire – Reverend Priest, 1813
Cambridge – Reverend Gooch, 1811
Cornwall – G. Worgan, 1811
Derbyshire – John Farey, 1817
Durham – John Bailey, 1813
Essex – Arthur Young, 1807
Hereford – John Duncumb, 1805
Lancashire – R. Dickson/W. Stephenson, 1815
Lancaster – John Holt, 1795
Leicester – W. Pitt, 1809
Middlesex – John Middleton, 1798
Northampton – W. Pitt, 1809
Rutland – R. Parkinson, 1808
Shropshire – Joseph Plymley, 1803
Somerset – John Thillingsley, 1798
Stafford – W. Pitt, 1796
Sussex – Arthur Young, 1817
East Riding – H. Strickland, 1812

Cobbett, William (1828). *Cottage Economy*, London.
Culley, George (1807). *Observations on Livestock*, London.
Davidson, H.R. (1966). *The Production and Marketing of Pigs*, Longmans, London.
Dictionarium Rusticum (1726). London.
Layley, G.W. & Malden, W.J. (1935). *Evolution of the British Pig*, J. Bolt, London.
Lawrence, John (1805). *A General Treatise on Cattle, the Ox, the Sheep*

and the Swine, London.

Long, James (1886). *The Book of the Pig*, London.

Loudon, John C. (1831). *An Encyclopaedia of Agriculture*, London.

Low, D. (1842). *The Breeds of the Domestic Animals of the British Isles*, London.

Markham, Gervase (1683). *Cheap and Good Husbandry*, London.

Marshall, William (1790). *The Rural Economy of the Midland Counties*, London.

Marshall, William (1796). *The Rural Economy of the West of England*, London.

Mills, John (1776). *A Treatise on Cattle*, Dublin.

Mortimer, John (1716). *The Whole Art of Husbandry*, London.

Spencer, Saunders (1919). *Pigs: breeds and management*, London.

Sydney, Samuel (1871). *The Pig*, London.

Trow-Smith, R. (1957). *A History of British Livestock Husbandry* (vols I & II), Routledge & Kegan Paul, London.

Tusser, Thomas (mid-16th century). *Points of Good Husbandry*, 1930 edition, E.V. Lucas, London.

Wilson, John M. (1847) *The Rural Cyclopaedia* (4 vols), Edinburgh.

Wright, P. (ed.) (1909) *Standard Cyclopaedia of Modern Agriculture* (12 vols). The pig entries were written by Saunders Spencer.

Youatt, W. (1847) *The Pig*.

Zeuner, F.E. (1963) *A History of Domesticated Animals*. Hutchinson, London.

Index